CW00541506

"Knowing when to break the rules, throwing caution to the wind in just the right way, is the sign of an evolved adult."

The birthday, page 102

the gentlewoman

Modern Manners

Instructions for living fabulously well

politely

How do we navigate those pitfalls of the modern world for which there are few precedents? With the right skills for the job, smart accoutrements and a carefully composed autoreply.

Out
of office

If the medium is the message, then what does an out-of-office really say, and what are the politics of a carefully composed autoreply?

By Susie Rushton

For years, whenever I went away, I would set an out-of-office reply that was perfectly to the point. "I am on holiday," it read, before naming another editor who might be contacted in my absence. Because honestly, I wanted the recipient to know I was not going to read her message — emails are work, and I wasn't working. Eventually a colleague intervened. My out-of-office was "hilarious", she told me, which is of course an English way of saying "rude". (But not as rude as that of the artists Gilbert and George. Their answering machine — they don't have email — signs off "Goodbye. And good riddance.") The thing is, I had to leave some sort of message — you can't ignore the one-sided drone of email. It goes on and on — to a degree that even Nora Ephron would have tired of eventually.

Availability — to one's work, to clients, to the latest urgent message from Deliveroo — has become relative. Leave an autoreply on your email and you'll be contacted via WhatsApp or text. Nobody is truly out of the office any more (or on holiday, for that matter; I was definitely showing my age). So the wording of an OoO is a rune to be deciphered. One is "away", "out" or possibly "travelling with limited access" — the last being the flimsiest excuse of all, given that most of Bhutan has 5G coverage.

What's become normal is to seem on-on-on, even when we also claim to be off. Lots of freelancers won't use an autoreply at all. Or if they do, it's another branding opportunity, a chance to redirect you to their Instagram feed or the press release for their latest novel, or to remind you that they're hot right now. "I am in the middle of a five-day trial," a barrister friend's OoO often reads, brooking no argument.

An inbox is like a nest of chicks with gaping soft beaks, each one waiting for a worm. An out-of-office isn't a worm, though: it's a promise of a worm. You promise to read the mail at a future date. This is almost always a lie. The email will no longer be relevant. It will be deleted. So why not tell the truth? Arianna Huffington, whose company, Thrive Global, promotes mindfulness and sells miniature beds for our phones — "First we tuck our phones in, then ourselves" — has developed an app, a "vacation email tool", that deletes incoming messages while you're on holiday, letting recipients know their emails won't be read.

Most of us could do with the occasional disconnect. I have a suggestion, therefore. We should no longer call it an OoO but more accurately call it a STFU — in the nicest possible way, of course. An elegant example is the message that bounces back to anyone who emails the publishing director James Roxburgh of Atlantic Books when he's on holiday. Currently, it reads: "I'm in Texas till Wednesday 1st and am entirely reluctant to access my emails. If it can't wait, then please do contact my colleague X." Roxburgh explains that the tart tone is "in defiance of the idea that we make ourselves permanently available. Of course, it's all self-inflicted, self-perpetuated and self-policed — we see another editor's 24-hour commitment in their out-of-offices and so feed the competitive need to be as heroically committed."

How you use your out-of-office says an awful lot about your general relationship with work. And those who take the "your email is being deleted" approach are probably highly productive and healthy. But there is a case for using the out-of-office more often, more strategically.

It buys you time, says Tina Preschitz, a producer, who uses it to screen emails, "because being a producer means also being a babysitter; you need to be reachable day and night. So I set an out-of-office when I can't answer for a period of time."

This set-up is close to ideal for those who want to min-imise interruption and deal with email effectively without seeming like an off-grid refusenik. But you could take it further and leave an unapologetically cryptic response for friends and colleagues, wrong-footing them into never bothering to email again. This is the reply Tilda Swinton bounces back: "Hello, I am away until 01/01/2070 and am unable to read your message."

Is Swinton heading out to orbit Mars? Cryogenically unavailable until further notice? Or was this just a key mis-stroke? I wondered via email.

She emails back, after a slight delay, to explain: "I looked at the email traffic and thought I should set a date by which I honestly thought I might be able to get back to everybody."

I'd like to think we can have a happy relationship with email, given everything it has enabled in the past three decades. But that might mean periodically shuttering the inbox, being straight about why we're doing so, and may-be even humanising the dead robotic message with a little of Tilda Swinton's charm — though half a century is a long wait for a reply, even from a movie star.

Diary

By Caroline Roux

At the start of my smartphone relationship, the diary function seemed to offer the best of every world. It soaked up details! It synced! It flagged up clashes with its blue boxes! But having reeled me in, it began to play games. First, it started to self-delete once the day was done. Looking back, I'd discover the backlit page glowing eerily empty, as though I had only imagined a life full of events and activities.

Then I started to arrive for appointments at the wrong time and on the wrong day. "What do you mean, we haven't got a booking?" I said — probably a little too icily — to the sleepy receptionist at the Social Eating House in London's Soho one Wednesday lunchtime. The booking turned out to be for the following day: so slippery is the scrolling function for date and time, I'd inadvertently moved my meeting back 24 hours. I missed a physio appointment; I was a day late for a private view, an hour out for a film screening. I began to worry I'd leave a significant interviewee hanging around in a hotel bar, while my digital diary continued to lead a fun if fictitious life of its own.

Finally, after seven increasingly problematic years, I gave in and headed to Smythson (a rare provider, it turned out, of soft, slim pocket diaries, as other stationers might like to note). Now a slender appointment book filled with delicate gold-edged pages is never far from my side. "Diary", it says (rather unnecessarily, if you ask me) on its navy blue leather cover. At least it doesn't have my initials.

I'm often surprised by how taken others are by its material presence when I whip it out of my bag and flick it open, making the pages chirrup; and I love the way I can look at a week of my life without so much as pressing a button. The day-to-day spaces might be small, but with a newly developed form of tiny writing, the services of an HB pencil complete with an eraser at its end (ink shows through the fine paper and isn't reversible), and both vertical and horizontal entries, it's easy to register the essentials. The details of complicated schedules — trips abroad, meetings with long agendas — never fitted into my phone, either.

Unlike my digital diary, which I thought would solve all life's problems instead of creating more, I regard my paper one purely as an aide-memoire. But in reality, it's already become something much more colourful — a treasure trove of phone numbers and other incidentals scribbled in the blank pages at back and front along with the odd doodle. It's rapidly acquiring a personality all its own, but not the kind that means I'll turn up at the wrong time on the wrong day.

This piece was written in 2015. The faults and slips in the digital diary have since been corrected.

New skills

We all want to be better versions of ourselves: more talented, more equipped, more accomplished. At least in our mind's eye, and ideally with as little investment as possible.

By Ann Friedman

My childhood piano teacher, Mrs Crowley, lived in a big wooden A-frame house on the outskirts of my small town. For an hour each week, I sat at her glossy black baby grand and sought the notes with my fingers. The room had high, sloped ceilings — all the way up to the peak of the frame — with old birdcages hanging from the rafters. And Mrs Crowley had the most beautiful bony hands. They looked disconcertingly alien on the keys, yet they moved with absolute certainty when she played for me at the end of my lesson.

I'm not sure exactly when I started romanticising those piano lessons. For most of the eight years I played, I was distinctly undisciplined about practising. As I got older, I thought for months about quitting until finally, when I was 14, I worked up the courage to tell Mrs Crowley I wouldn't be coming back. By the time I went away to college, I couldn't play a single song. But a few years ago, I started thinking about taking piano lessons again. I love music, but that wasn't my main motivation. I craved the lessons themselves — the relief of agreed-upon rules when real life can be so chaotic. At a lesson there is a correct order in which to do things, a tried-and-tested process for improvement, and clear benchmarks for measuring progress.

Adult enrichment courses and hobbyist classes are nothing new, but there seems to be an acute hunger for learning these days. In our age of find-your-own-way relationships and careers that no longer resemble the metaphorical ladder, the pleasures of explicit instruction are real. Plenty is available online, and much of it relates to decidedly non-digital pursuits such as pickling, fabric painting and calligraphy, to name just a few of the topics that have caught my eye lately. I'm not the only one who's been tempted to enrol: 55 per cent of Americans aged between 30 and 39 say they've watched online videos to learn a new art or craft. And there are endless ways in which to acquire that skill. The monthly subscription service Skillshare offers users more than 27,000 classes on a huge range of subjects as diverse as flower arranging, DIY and wholesale importing from China. MasterClass grants access to hundreds of experts and celebrities, including Aaron Sorkin, Werner Herzog and Serena Williams, who offer instruction in their fields. And the novice home cook has at her disposal endless YouTube tutorials about the best way to slice an onion or poach a pear. It's never been easier to broaden one's skill set.

Of course signing up for instruction requires admitting to a certain level of ignorance. To take lessons is to nudge oneself into discomfort. When you need something explained again, or when you just can't get your fingers to do what they're supposed to, humility is a requirement. And the older one gets, the easier it becomes not to put oneself in such situations, to stay within the well-defined boundaries of experience and competence, and the harder it is to learn. A Brown University study found that older adults have a harder time processing and sorting relevant details from irrelevant ones and end up absorbing more information than is necessary to focus on the task at hand. But researchers at the University of Texas have confirmed that "mentally-challenging leisure activities" can restore the brain to "a more youth-like state".

Even with a compelling argument in favour of lessons, they can be difficult to shoehorn into the diary. As a self-employed writer, I find it hard to turn down assignments, and as a consequence I've watched my work days grow longer and longer. I'm not drawn to learning out of boredom. I've got nothing in common with the housewife of decades past, who might have taken a cookery course in order to throw impressive dinner parties for her husband's colleagues. And it's not that I'm unchallenged either. In recent years I've purchased books and downloaded apps that promised, respectively, to help me to bake a decent loaf of bread from scratch and learn basic French. Each came with explicit instructions and clear steps. Yet I was never very good at making time to follow them — perhaps I would have been if I'd enrolled in a baking class or signed up for group language lessons. Accountability in numbers is, for many, the key to instructional success.

I decided that to commit, what I needed was a weekly one-on-one date with a teacher. And taking up piano again was a tantalising idea. I saw myself closing my laptop at the end of the working day and opening the piano lid to place my fingers on an entirely different set of keys. My boyfriend had brought his Clavinova electric piano with him when he'd moved in with me a few years ago. It seemed a shame not to use it, and practising posed the perfect antidote to my personal dilemmas and professional stress. And, I confess, I had a fantasy of delighting my tipsy friends with the opening notes of "Tiny Dancer", prompting a jovial singalong on a Saturday night. I looked forward to casually mentioning to acquaintances that I was taking piano lessons, too. Even more than a meditation app or a Pilates trainer, adult music instruction conveys a studious commitment to self-enrichment.

I knew I would need another Mrs Crowley, someone who would inspire both a love of music and the motivation to practise it. Her name is Rose. (When you're an adult, you get to call your teacher by her first name.) For the past five months, we've been meeting about once a week in her small second-floor apartment in Mar Vista, on the west side of Los Angeles. There are no birdcages, but there is a cream-coloured upright piano with flaking paint that's been in her family for generations.

Adult learners, she told me, tend to bore easily with the classic sight-reading approach to piano lessons. Instead, she instructed me to bring in songs I like. Now I hold up my phone and press play so Rose can hear the first several bars of a song. She finds the notes on the piano and teaches me the chords. Mostly they're old soul numbers — Sam Cooke, Ike and Tina. We tried a Kate Bush song one week, but after I utterly failed to pluck out the complex chords of "Babooshka", she gently steered me back to simpler sounds.

I trust her methods — isn't that the point of paying a teacher? But I'm insecure. The process has been one big question: am I doing it right? And it comes with lots of sub-questions. Have I chosen the right teacher? Am I bringing her the right songs? Are lessons a waste of my money? What am I really getting out of this?

Part of the appeal of the piano is that if my fingers are busy finding the chords, they can't be tapping out text messages. But both my attention span and my sense of productivity have been compromised by the hours I spend online, and I'm ashamed to admit how quickly I get bored practising the same notes over and over. And even though

I knew I was starting virtually from scratch, I thought I would be better. So I have to rein in my expectations. This has been the most difficult part of the process.

Perhaps it's why I've reverted to my childhood habit of cramming in an hour of practice right before I drive across town to Rose's, which is a bit rich considering that a major reason I wanted to take piano lessons was that I thought it would be relaxing to sit and play for a little while each day. Any progress is hard-won, yet the rewards are almost imperceptibly small. Although I once looked forward to telling friends I'd taken up the piano again, now I go out of my way not to mention it: I'm terrified that someone is going to produce a keyboard and ask me to play. They'd hear six chords of Sam Cooke's "Nothing Can Change This Love" played by my stiff fingers.

It's so easy to forget the insecurity that comes with being a beginner, even in such a low-stakes context as adult music lessons. For all the progress I've made in my life, in this particular area I'm less accomplished than I was when I was 12. On occasion, though, I've found myself lost in practice. This is when the questions disappear. My daily anxieties around trying to do several things at once are gone, too. I'm not answering an email while half-listening in on a conference call, or making dinner while watching the news. It's just me, my hands, the keys. And in that concentration, I find pleasure that's real, both deeper and sweeter than the individual notes.

The folding coat hanger

By Penny Martin

There are plenty of ways to hang up a coat, and depending on the garment, quite a few of them will do it no favours. Sling a nice new double-face cashmere one onto a hook just below its collar and find a freshly minted hump in the fabric just a couple of hours later. Use one of those pretty little hanging chains stitched at the nape of the neck and risk a lining that has parted company with its outer layer.

If it sounds a little fastidious to worry about such things, consider the cost. Many people spend about a fifth of their annual clothing budget on a coat, which, regardless of the scale of the budget, makes it an expensive item.

Yet we can be remarkably cavalier with the priciest of things. While a £1,000 watch will always be handled with exquisite care, how many times is a £2,000 handbag dumped onto a floor? An iPad (£400) is never thrown around, but a jumper (also £400) frequently gets bundled into a bag. (It might not be breakable, but knitwear is fragile in its own way.) Scarves, gloves, sought-after designer wallets — all of these are subjected to their own unique indignities.

And coats? Hung, flung, trailing off the back of a chair... Abuse comes in many forms. One way to care more is to invest in a folding coat hanger. This perfect piece of domestic design has remained unchanged since it was first devised in the 1920s for use in railroad sleeping cars, ocean liners and aircraft. Some versions are customised with brushes and padding and even impregnated with fragrance, but their purpose has stayed the same: to keep garments pristine in transit, then collapse into the tiniest possible size upon arrival.

The only question is how the folding coat hanger should be introduced into a modern public situation, such as a contemporarily spartan restaurant where waiters have been taught to suspend coats on those school-cloakroom-style pegs that bristle their way around the walls. Should the opened hanger be slipped quietly into the coat before handover commences, or produced brazenly from its carrying bag as if unsheathing a sword? That's a matter of personal style.

But don't forget to retrieve it along with the coat upon departure — these little gadgets are surprisingly covetable.

Silver beaker

By Mark Smith

In the wake of global calamity, tall talk from the top — of wide-reaching reform and sweeping structural sea change — is often accompanied, and ultimately outlived, by smaller, behavioural adjustments that can be enacted by lots of individuals on a habitual basis. Profane as it sounds, for many Europeans the War on Liquids of More than 100ml has proven more consuming than its ideological progenitor, the War on Terror. After all, its spectre returns every time we decant conditioner into an infuriating miniature bottle for a cabin-baggage-only business trip or witness the merciless airport confiscation of a fellow holidaymaker's egregious magnitudes of Balsamico di Modena.

Covid-19 has wrought countless quotidian changes already, but perhaps one of those enduring small behavioural adjustments is Bring Your Own Utensils, whereby revellers supply their own cutlery and drinking vessels at events both public and private, indoors and out.

Ostensibly a measure to evade the pathological perils of shared hardware, BYOU also affords an opportunity to purchase the reassuringly expensive and endlessly exquisite Puiforcat silver champagne tumbler for spontaneous toasting. Stowed concealed-carry-style, ready to emerge from your handbag at the merest whiff of a knees-up, it brings the festive aesthetics of the condensation-dappled silver ice bucket and does a similar job in keeping one's drink cool.

The BYOU movement has myriad antecedents, of course. Ultra-observant Jews are used to packing kosher tackle for eating abroad. The actor and swimwear tycoon Elizabeth Hurley has long been rumoured to arrive at functions with a tiny knife-and-fork set because it makes every bite look bigger, thus aiding effective portion control. And an excursion to London's Bermondsey Market on any given Friday will reveal all manner of "campaign" cutlery — from pearl-handled Georgian fruit knives which fold up like a Swiss Army knife to Ottoman sherbet spoons and Chinese bone chopsticks in finely carved sheaths. Old solutions to new problems, then, from times when being catered to was not always a given.

What was your first job?

A gentlewoman has to start somewhere. In 2018, 36 women of distinction were asked to share their tales from the trenches of the working world by responding to the question, "What was your first job?"

MIRANDA JULY (artist, Los Angeles) "I got a job at a produce market in Berkeley, California, called Del Tomaso; I was 16. Each fruit and vegetable had its own code — I can still remember bananas were 11, which seemed to have a visual logic."

KIRSTY WARK (broadcaster, Glasgow) "At 14 I worked in a gift shop in my home town of Kilmarnock in East Ayrshire. It was owned by a Danish family and stocked pieces of teak furniture and Georg Jensen jewellery — this was 1969. In Scotland."

HONEY DIJON (DJ and music producer, New York) "My dad managed a chain of drugstores, so at 16 I got a post refilling shelves at our local one in the suburbs of south Chicago. This was pre-digital, so I had to walk around noting missing items, locate them in the stockroom and refill the shelves. For six hours a day, six days a week."

LUCY McKENZIE (artist, Brussels) "The owner of a pharmacy in Glasgow offered me a job as a signwriter when he saw me sketching the interior of Queen Street train station. I was 16, and I guess the qualifications for the post were being arty and cheap."

SHIRIN NESHAT (artist, New York) "When I was a student at Berkeley in the late 1970s, I worked in a flower shop. I loved it."

SUSIE CAVE (designer, Brighton) "I swept floors at a hairdresser's in south-east London called the Hair Inn. I was 14 and absolutely loved it. It was opposite Chislehurst Caves, where the actor Sylvia Syms was filming at the time. She used to come into the salon — I could hardly breathe. That's where my near-religious devotion to hair began."

ALICE RAWSTHORN (design critic, London) "In sixth form, I was a Saturday girl at Boots in Braintree, Essex. We had fun blowing up condoms for stockroom balloon fights."

LYNN BARBER (journalist, London) "My first job was at *Penthouse* magazine. I was paid £16 a week, which was good money in 1966 — *Vogue* had only offered me £12."

PRINCESS JULIA (nightclub legend, London) "In 1976, I started as a hairdresser's apprentice at Crimpers in Knightsbridge. Though I was the height of punk, it was all flicked fringes, zhooshy hair and highlights. Quite the contradiction. I once lost a client's diamond earring down the plughole giving her a shampoo."

FRANCES MORRIS (director, Tate Modern, London) "As a postgrad, I couriered sacks of plasma and other unlikely, but probably life-saving, products on planes across Europe."

HILARY MANTEL (writer, Sunningdale) "After finishing my degree, I had intended to be a lawyer, but I couldn't afford to go on with the training, so I joined the social work team in a geriatric hospital. The surroundings were grim; many of our patients remembered when it had been the town workhouse. It was a useful job, practical, and it didn't depress me, though I learned gruesome things about the human mind and body that a 21-year-old shouldn't have to know."

VERONICA DITTING (creative director, London) "1999 was the year of the first *Star Wars* prequel, and that was my hook to sell Premiere World's digital TV package in a shopping mall in Bochum, north-west Germany. I stood on a plastic dais, wearing a red T-shirt, extolling the virtues of a black set-top box. German men love technology, so I was quite successful."

JESSICA SEATON (founder, Toast, Nevern, Wales) "I was a fledgling archaeologist, spending my days scraping the soil away from a suspected Iron Age fort on an exposed hill above the sea in south Wales. There were no finds whatsoever, which we all found hilarious, but I learned valuable life skills such as landing a shovelful of soil into a wheelbarrow at 10 paces."

KATHARINE HAMNETT (designer, London) "Hop picking in Kent, when I was 13. I earned £6 17s 6d in total — about £105 today — for a 12-hour day, six days a week. I realised this wasn't the job for me."

SUSIE DENT (etymologist and lexicographer, Oxfordshire) "I waited tables in a wine bar near Windsor. I have profound memories of garlic — the staff were allowed to eat from the menu, so I ploughed my way through entire loaves of garlic bread, followed by huge mouthfuls of parsley, which was supposed to mask the smell. I don't think I fooled anyone, least of all one visiting politician, who commented that I could clearly recommend one item on the menu."

SUSANNA LAU (fashion blogger, London) "I did stocktaking for Stanley Gibbons and Fraser's Autographs on the Strand. It involved counting thousands of stamps and ensuring every autograph and piece of celebrity memorabilia was accounted for. They sold George Washington's hair for £500 a strand."

ELIZABETH PEYTON (artist, New York) "The first summer after I moved to New York City to attend the School of Visual Arts in 1982, I got a job as a walking messenger. All I had to do was turn up and show I was able-bodied. It taught me where the best public toilets are in New York. FYI: the Plaza."

HANNAH MacGIBBON (designer, London) "Driven by my obsession with clothes, I took a Saturday job in a clothes shop in Chapel Market, north London, to pay for them. I was 15 and wasn't cut out to be a salesperson — a day seemed like a week. We'd play Gwen Guthrie's "Ain't Nothin' Goin' On but the Rent" at full volume on repeat. I didn't last very long."

KITTY TRAVERS (CEO, La Grotta Ices, London) "I worked on a milk float with a perverted milkman."

What was your first job?

MOLLY GODDARD (designer, London) "I taught football to primary-school kids at an after-school club."

SALI HUGHES (beauty writer, Brighton and London) "My first break was as first assistant to the late, great make-up artist Lynne Easton. We met in 1990, when I was 15 and wearing some wildly inappropriate transparent top, hot pants and biker boots in Fred's bar in Soho. She had the same top on, and we got chatting. Day one was a commercial for Lindt chocolate: I had to make 40 extras look like different Hollywood icons. Day two was a Pet Shop Boys video, then a George Michael shoot, and we were off."

PENNY MARTIN (editor, London) "Desperate to work at Rumplesilkskin, the new bridal shop in St Andrews, I sent the two shopkeepers a ghost story I had written featuring them. Somehow, that creepy overture convinced them to employ me for £1.75 an hour. My days of fitting satin shoes and carrying veils were short-lived, though. A raucous try-on session with friends in the back room caused a bride-to-be to complain about the noise and we lost the sale of an Edwardian-style silk gown by Mr Gubbins."

MARTINE ROSE (designer, London) "There was a call centre on an industrial estate in Redhill, Surrey, and I worked there selling cruises. It involved cold-calling pensioners, and I absolutely hated it.

MARINA O'LOUGHLIN (restaurant critic, London) "Straight from an aborted university attempt I started working as a waitress in Glasgow. I felt as if I'd finally found my tribe: hard-working, hard-drinking, hard-partying people. I made lifelong friends — and developed a healthy wariness of chefs."

CHARLIE BRINKHURST-CUFF (journalist, London) "Working in a toyshop is not fun for a 16-year-old. It was a yellow-painted hell-hole, stuffed with sticky screaming children who, on a couple of memorable occasions, shit on the floor. But I stayed there for almost four years. I'm excellent at buying gifts for children."

VAL McDERMID (writer, Edinburgh) "I was a silver-service waitress at the Station Hotel in Kirkcaldy. Unless you were really skilled, peas would fly everywhere, and chips could only be transferred two or three at a time. The order we all dreaded was grilled trout. The fish was delivered to the table whole, and after displaying it to the customer, we had to remove the head and fillet it at the table, then get it on the plate in one piece."

RUTH CHAPMAN (entrepreneur, London) "I got my start working in an old ladies' knickers and tights shop. Trade was slow, and customers spent hours feeling fabrics, trying things on. I was always up a ladder, finding specific brassieres, corsets, deniers... I was 13. It was quite an eye-opener, let me tell you."

ROKSANDA ILINČIĆ (designer, London) "An advertising agency back home in Belgrade wanted an unusual poster for a watch company and it approached the local art colleges to get students to submit designs. Mine must have been too unusual — it never materialised."

JAE CHOI (agent, New York) "As an airport concierge, I met VIP clients of a limousine company at the arrivals gate or escorted them from kerbside to departures, all the while in constant communication with the driver by walkie-talkie. Cheese and crackers in the lounge with Robert Downey Jr. at 16? Not too shabby."

MONIKA LINTON (founder, and owner Brindisa, London) "Early on, I worked at the Big Box toy company on Alton industrial estate in Hampshire, packing Ladybird domino sets and other games. I have to admit that it wasn't particularly challenging."

ALLISON JANNEY (actor, Los Angeles) "By day, I scooped ice cream and by night I was a receptionist at a recording studio."

LUCIA PICA (global creative make-up and colour designer, Chanel, Paris and London) "I got a summer job collecting glasses in a huge open-air nightclub. I was 16, but my older brother worked there, so as far as everyone was concerned I was supervised! I had the best time."

LOUISE TROTTER (designer, London and Paris) "From 16, I worked in a mechanic's garage. My ability to accurately measure the pigment for spray jobs for all manner of vehicles meant I was soon promoted to chief mixer. I spent that summer with my hands permanently dyed Fiesta red."

YASMIN LE BON (model, London) "At 13 or 14, I looked about 35 with my hair slicked back, a full face of make-up and high heels. So my brother-in-law got me a job as a cashier in the men's clothes shop he managed. I was in charge of the till and cashing up; I developed a taste for power quite early on. I loved clothes and I loved selling — so nothing's changed there."

PAULA GERBASE (designer, London) "When I was seven and living in Baltimore, Maryland, I set up a pickle stand. A few neighbourhood kids had lemonade stands, which seemed impressively profitable, judging by the amounts of Fruit Roll-Ups they were able to buy at the local store. So I recruited our teenage babysitter as chief pickle maker. Given her limited skills, pickled cucumbers were my only option. Needless to say, not many sold, and I've had an aversion to pickles ever since."

SALLY PHILLIPS (actor, London) "I worked in the mailroom at Oxford City Council, under the control of the office services manager. I did a lot of carrying stationery boxes between floors, to a running commentary from two guys in overalls sat in reception. At the end of the week I typed out their names and job titles on pay packets. I was fired for insubordination soon after. The name of the office services manager (including middle initial) featured quite a lot in *Smack the Pony*."

2.

What are the new rules for the old problems of socialising solo, receiving and giving gifts and absolving oneself of gaffes for which no words can atone?

Modern

conun-
drums

Arriving alone

By Caroline Roux

Certain types of job can lead to any number of party and dinner invitations, from the dazzling to the do-I-have-to. Working in the arty part of the media certainly does: exhibition openings, fashion parties, intimate suppers in private rooms, vast dinners in the echoing galleries of national museums, cocktails at collectors' mansions, screenings by swimming pools, warm wine in an architect's new office are all on offer. It's delightful, of course. And then again, it's not. Often the invitation is for one, signified by those chilling words "admits one, strictly non-transferable". Is this a friendly request for one's company or a set of instructions?

After years of enforced solo socialising, I've developed some rules for the uncomfortable situation of arriving alone. First, carry a small bag and wear a light coat. It's best to avoid leaving items in the cloakroom; it can slow down a fast getaway. Next, perfect the U-shaped room tour. This involves a hasty sweep through those present, assessing the ratio of friendly to adored versus dull to toxic. If there's not one familiar face (and, really, that can happen), effect an instant departure. The less time spent in the room, the easier it is to leave.

At a very busy event, it's helpful to consider the defining characteristics of those it would be most fun to find. One recent summer I found myself at a fabulous but overrun art opening in New York, lost among hundreds of unfamiliar faces. The Brits, I decided, would most likely gravitate to the bar. They did — quite possibly all of them. It was a good night.

And then there's smoking. I know, I know. But desperate situations warrant desperate measures. Peering into an iPhone suggests self-conscious isolation; standing alone for a languorous smoke is a far better look. Within seconds, someone who has "given up" or needs a light will approach. And that's the beauty of arriving alone. Being devoid of an old friend makes room for a new one.

Regifting

By Anna-Marie Solowij

The days when journalists (and indeed anyone in politics, hospitality and many other professions) were plied with gifts may be on the wane. But if I'd kept everything I'd ever received (as a former beauty editor, I used to get an awful lot), I'd need an industrial-sized storage unit to house it all. Surely, I persuade myself, it's better to spread the ridiculously good fortune and pass on the excess gifts to others? Or should one feel guilty about giving away the fruits of other people's generosity while at the same time perhaps cheapening the value of the gift to the receiver by dint of making it second-hand?

Curiously, I find the receipt of an explicitly expensive gift is both boon and burden: does its value mean I'm obliged to keep it forever, or should I take delight in being able to pass it on to a new owner less spoiled than I? And if I do decide to regift — for me, the prospect of empty cupboards trumps a collection of hardware-heavy handbags every time — should I explain that I didn't pay for it? In which case, is it still officially a gift, or is there a requirement for some new nomenclature — a pift (passed-on gift), a nift (no-longer-wanted gift) or, God forbid, a rift?

I can't help feeling I've fallen foul of my misplaced generosity in the past by handing on gifts that I couldn't possibly afford to buy in the first place. My sister recently asked if I had "any more of those Chanel sunglasses", her tone implying that I had shedloads of them just waiting to be tossed in her direction. I had regifted a pair for her birthday and she had subsequently lost them. Because she knew I hadn't actually paid for them, I think she valued them less, so felt able to tell me of their loss as well as to ask for a replacement pair. I guess I can't criticise; if I didn't want them, then why should she value them greatly?

Now I've found the only way I can conscionably regift is by adding value — giving another very carefully chosen gift, which I've obviously paid for, on top of the regift. The result is somewhat schizophrenic: cashmere track suit and narcissus bulbs for my mother; electronic facelifting machine and frying pan for sister one; designer travel bag and vintage ceramic plant pot for sister two. But the outcome is, I hope, satisfactory for all: they get something they wouldn't buy for themselves or receive from anyone else, and I get relatively uncluttered cupboards and complete alleviation of guilt.

The solitary drink

In a bygone era, the bar was the last refuge of the single or pack male. Modern women have changed that. Initial infiltration was conducted in groups, but now certain individuals are going it alone.

By Ann Friedman

Drinking alone has long been regarded as the domain of the socially inept and the hopelessly addicted, a sad occurrence one certainly didn't wish to see acted out in public. But for once, I find myself agreeing with Christopher Hitchens. "It's not true that you shouldn't drink alone," the scotch-loving critic wrote. "These can be the happiest glasses you ever drain." Indeed, if conducted in moderation and in view of others, there's no reason solo drinking shouldn't be a blameless pastime for the socially confident and self-reflective.

For some, a quiet drink by oneself can create a peaceful period of transition — from day to evening, from professional to social. For the connoisseur, it's the perfect opportunity to appreciate every smoky note of an 18-year-old Laphroaig or the delicious mouthfeel of a Cotes du Rhône. And sometimes it's less about what's in the glass than who's doing the sipping. A woman enjoying the pleasure of her own company at the bar exudes a certain sophistication: independence and enjoyment intermingled with a whiff of reserve. She's like the woman rewarding herself with a single slice of cake or sneaking off to the cinema on her own, untroubled by the judgement of others and clear about her priorities. It's a long way from a boisterous night out on the lash with the girls, more a moment of self-indulgent pleasure.

I've found again and again that Hitchens was correct. But to get to these happy glasses, a bit of a learning curve was required. I had to convince myself that heading to a bar alone wasn't desperate or pathetic. I had to find the right establishment for my first solo outings. I had to set my own pace and sip slowly; resist the urge to bask in the glow of that modern chaperone, the iPhone; not care whether other patrons noticed I was unaccompanied. It turned out that drinking alone was a low-stakes lesson in independence and composure, allowing me to hone the art of appearing comfortable in my own skin until I really was.

There are a few other hurdles to clear, too. Across cultures — from cities in Sweden to Gypsy camps in Hungary and villages in northern Laos — studies have found universal condemnation of the act of drinking alone, according to the Social Issues Research Centre, a non-profit organisation based in Oxford, in a report presented to the EU. Because drinking is seen as a social act, solitary consumption suggests alcoholism, or at the very least an inability to cope with one's problems. It's somehow assumed that alcohol's more malign qualities are neutered somewhat when it is shared. And buying a round isn't just a show of camaraderie; it's the initiation of a bond in which all parties agree not to judge each other for what happens next.

The solo drinker is extended no such assurances, and this is especially true for a woman. As recently as a couple of decades ago, an unescorted female in a bar was assumed to be a loser — stood up by her date — or a prostitute. Even if she wasn't visibly intoxicated, in the absence of a man, her very presence was suspect. Go back further and women, expected to be guardians of morality and emblems of self-control, couldn't be seen imbibing at all. In Prohibition-era America, the Woman's Christian Temperance Union had the dual goals of curtailing alcohol consumption and pushing for women's suffrage, arguing that women were morally opposed to drinking and could therefore be trusted to vote wisely.

While groups of women, even extremely drunk ones, are now considered unexceptional, there remains a lingering bias. In 2004, researchers analysed decades of British newspaper coverage of women and drinking. A woman with a drink in her hand, they found, "is positioned as vulnerable but also partially responsible for any harm that she suffers, as drinking women are often viewed as sexually promiscuous."

And there's no reason to think things have changed. Even today, opinion columnists, armed with statistics on the number of sexual assaults in which one or both parties are drunk, utilise this finger-wagging at careless young women who venture out to drink, alone or otherwise, warning that it makes them seem unladylike at best and easy targets at worst. And lest we forget, there are physiological differences that do make drinking more dangerous for women than for men: women tend to be smaller, process alcohol differently and get drunk more quickly. Drinking in anything but small quantities is bad for us all.

So let me clarify one point: drinking alone, when done correctly, is not about getting drunk, or even tipsy. I'm far more responsible on my solo drinking excursions. When I think of all the times I've had one or three too many, it's most often been because my friends are ordering another round, because I was caught up in conversation and lost track of how many times my glass had been refilled, or because I was trying to work up the courage to lean in for a kiss. Alone, I've felt no such pressure and have never lost count.

Accomplished solo drinking requires savvy and self-control. It's not for women who tipple until they topple.

Slowly and steadily, each sip relaxes me, signifies the end of the working day, and helps me move on to a new headspace before I settle in for the evening. When *The Paris Review* asked Joan Didion about her most important writing ritual, she replied that she took "an hour alone before dinner, with a drink, to go over what I've done that day."

In order for one to credibly claim this act as one of deliberate self-assurance rather than insecure deviance, ritual and rules matter, and I relish them. Week nights are best for solo drinking. I choose a low-key pub or a bar, ideally somewhere I've been before, with friendly bartenders and warm lighting, and I show up early in the evening when the staff are still wiping down the bar and restocking the pint glasses. If there's a corner or a short end of the bar, that's my spot. It allows me a fine view all the way down the long end, so I can see the faces of the other patrons — a perspective normally restricted to the bartender, and one that provides me with reliable entertainment should I choose to let my eyes wander.

If I'm feeling stressed and need to unwind, I order a single Templeton Rye whiskey, poured neat in a squat tumbler. If I'm planning to meet friends for dinner or at a party later, I frequently request a dry gin martini with three olives to slide off the toothpick with my teeth at the beginning, middle and end of my drink. If I'm already calm or headed home for the night, I'll opt for a generous pour of pinot noir, reflecting on the day with each circle of my wrist as I swirl the wine in the glass. (This also removes the possibility of opening a bottle at home for that one delightful pre-dinner glass and finding it drained by the end of the evening.)

No matter which drink I select, in each deliberate mouthful I find respite from the digital and social worlds. I try to keep my phone in my bag. I like being by myself with my thoughts. And I've come to enjoy the questioning looks from strangers who recognise the confidence required to pull off this minor social transgression without feeling threatened or cheapened by their gazes. I confess, too, that as a natural busybody, I love being in a public place with lots to observe. At the bar alone, I'm in a natural position to eavesdrop. I once listened to a middle-aged man explain to his date why he found waterskiing so erotic.

Drinking alone may be an independent pursuit, but it's far from antisocial. A special camaraderie with the bartender is, in fact, best developed solo. It's also a safeguard against the sorts of dangers we were raised to believe befall women who drink alone. There's a special protective bond that forms between bartenders and their solo patrons. Should the man on the next stool fail to listen when I tell him I'm just here to enjoy my glass of wine, the bartender will usually intervene on my behalf. These happy returns multiply with each visit to the same establishment. The staff become familiar with me — which brings its own comfort and safety — and with my preferences. They greet me with a nod, ask if I'll be having whiskey or wine (the martinis are a rare indulgence), and know that I'd also like a glass of water with no ice. What does a woman want more than to have her unspoken desires reliably met? A bartender can be trained more easily than a lover — after all, he works for tips.

Sorry

By Seb Emina

While public expressions of regret have become a mainstay of contemporary life, the evolving etiquette surrounding personal apologies is strangely underdiscussed. With modern life comes a proliferating catalogue of new ways to land oneself in a red-faced predicament (I'm sorry I pressed "Reply all", I'm sorry I retweeted your ex, I'm sorry I posted that video of you shuffle dancing), desperate for forgiveness, trying to find the words that enable re-entry to the fold.

Of course, the fundamental principles as to what makes a good versus a bad apology do not change even as the world evolves. The rule of Susan McCarthy, the founder of the website SorryWatch, that you must never follow "I'm sorry" with an "if" is correct whether the apology is uploaded to social media or tensely delivered over tea.

"I'm sorry if my killing your frog caused you pain" is wrong, McCarthy wrote in a landmark 2001 article. "I'm sorry I killed your frog" is best. Take responsibility.

The difference between saying sorry in public and in private relates less to what's said than to the medium of saying it. There are a million media to screw up in, but almost none of them is appropriate for making amends. It's impossible to deliver an effective apology, no matter how sincerely worded, via the chat box in the Scrabble app.

But is email all right? Text message? What about a phone call? Sorry not to give all the answers, but there's a point where the rules run out and you have to make a judgement. There is something sociopathic about following apology guidelines (many exist online) as if they're a recipe for risotto. Sincerity is key. Still, there are misdemeanours — forgetting certain birthdays, heinous but unavoidable cancellations — where electronic messaging is most likely acceptable. Meanwhile, if I break your nice vase, the verbal papering-over to follow will always be insufficient, no matter what I say. It's best to send something as a subsequent gesture, but what? "If you cannot afford to replace what you have broken or have it mended," the etiquette columnist Drusilla Beyfus suggested in the 1950s, "send a token of your apologies — flowers are better than silence." That's an easy example, and it holds firm 65 years hence. The mistake was simple, honest clumsiness: a quintessential flower-giving situation.

And there are the real humdingers: the weddings ruined, the cars written off, the bad things blurted. Pixel-based messaging is less useful here, and flowers and other tokens seem not so much sweet as avoiding the real issue. At the top of the pyramid we find two options: the handwritten letter and the face-to-face meeting. The former allows the apologiser to articulate their regret and the apologisee to sit with it a while. But there's a danger in being too eloquent. "I think it has to feel as if there is real emotion there," the bestselling author Naomi Alderman says. "Too much intellectualising or fine phrases can feel like it's avoiding emotion."

With an in-person meeting comes the benefit of, well, actual humiliation, which can feel as if the ceiling is caving in yet is usefully cathartic. "A face-to-face apology is such a classic place where we learn empathy," the social scientist Sherry Turkle, an expert on tech-derived malaise, has said. It is also an opportunity to work through the thing fully, an apology being ideally a one-off occasion (lest it descend into grovelling of a sort that needs itself to be apologised for).

Apologising is easy, except when it's important. The classic mistake is to lose perspective and forget to ask the most important question at all: what would I expect in their situation? If this question is considered honestly, the answer is often difficult and awkward, but actually not that complicated.

What were you doing 10 years ago?

To celebrate the publication of its tenth issue in 2014, The Gentlewoman found occasion to ask 24 much-admired women what they had been doing 10 years previously. 2004, it turned out, was filled with beginnings, endings and many moments of sheer delight.

KYLIE MINOGUE (singer, London) "I was promoting my album *Body Language*. It was all opaque tights and Bardot hair. I was ecstatic about the song "Slow" and the video we filmed at the Olympic pool in Barcelona. I also performed my one-night Money Can't Buy concert in London for an invited audience. It was a great success, but it did nearly tip us all over the edge. Ha! I was wildly in love, living between London and Paris, and everything seemed possible."

RUTH ROGERS (co-founder, River Café, London) "I remember listening rapt to a young African-American senator called Barack Obama speaking at the Democratic convention about the despair of people living in poverty. The same year was the wedding of our son Roo and Bernie Huang in Vernazza in the Cinque Terre. That was one of those magic days: Bernie was still in her bikini an hour before the ceremony. The local mayor did the honours in the piazza, and the whole town came, dancing till dawn, when boats came to take everyone away."

VICKY FEATHERSTONE (artistic director, Royal Court Theatre, London) "I was moving up to Glasgow with my husband, and five- and three-year-old kids to set up the National Theatre of Scotland. I was the first artistic director; my first day in the job involved sitting on the floor in a rented office with a notebook, no company bank account and no staff. Since then, NTS has made over 130 shows, played to over a million people worldwide and employed hundreds of actors, writers and artists. What an adventure!"

CYNTHIA PLASTER CASTER (artist, Chicago) "My highlight of 2004 was when the British filmmaker Lawrence Barraclough came to Chicago to interview me for the documentary he was making about having a small penis. As a film subject, it impressed me so much that I asked Lawrence to pose for me so that I could include him in my plaster collection of super-talented people's penises, along with Jimi Hendrix et al."

ALIONA DOLETSKAYA (former editor-in-chief, *Vogue* Russia, *Interview* Russia and Germany, Moscow) "What a year it was! I was the editor of *Vogue* Russia. The economy in Russia was so healthy; I had to come up with 500 pages monthly. The most fun was shooting covers with Karl Lagerfeld, including one with the 16-year-old, totally unknown Natasha Poly. I also shot a *Fight Club*-inspired story with the gold and silver world medal gymnasts Alina Kabaeva and Irina Tchachina. Alina went on to become the partner of President Putin and a member of parliament."

FRANCES VON HOFMANN-STHAL (editor and creative director, London) "I was 24, living in Paris and assisting Paolo Roversi. He would use me to do the light tests before the model arrived — I'd learned how to sit very still for photographs from my father, Snowdon. When I returned to London in late 2004, Paolo made me a little booklet of all the Polaroid tests that he had done with me: five years of different outfits — pink bows in my hair, safety pins in my tights, flea-market suits and dresses — and always the same grumpy, very still face."

JUDY MURRAY (tennis coach, Dunblane, Scotland) "In August 2004, I was the national coach for Scotland, and my son Andy was in Rome for a men's Futures tournament — that's the first level of the men's ATP World Tour. He was 17 years old. He won, against the odds, playing in front of a very noisy, partisan Italian crowd. From there, we headed to New York with his brother, Jamie, and Jamie Baker to get ready for the US Open juniors. To have three Scots in the draw at a junior Grand Slam was unheard of, and we got doubles semi-finalists and a boys' singles champion. We returned home to a pack of snappers at Edinburgh airport and a press squad on the drive of our house. Life has never quite been the same since."

What were you doing 10 years ago?

PAM HOGG (designer and DJ, London) "Ten years ago, Siouxsie Sioux asked me to design and make the costumes for her Dreamshow tour. I didn't even have a sewing machine — the person who I had asked to look after all my equipment until I decided to return to fashion had sold everything and disappeared. I was hosting clubs, too, including Slinky Salon, where people like Bobby Gillespie, Róisín Murphy and Boy George would get up and sing. Jarvis Cocker did a great "Devil Gate Drive" one night. He couldn't remember it the next day."

LAUREN COLLINS (writer, Paris) "Ten years ago, I was living on King Street in New York in a sixth-floor walk-up that didn't have an oven, eating a lot of Chipotle chicken burrito bowls (hold the guac!), using Hotmail, dry-cleaning my boot-cut jeans, occasionally dating a man with a tattoo of the comedy and drama masks, and trying to figure out why everyone was so upset about seeing Janet Jackson's nipple."

SINÉAD O'CONNOR (singer, Bray, Ireland) "It was the year my now 10-year-old son, Shane, was born. He arrived two weeks early, on his father's and sister's birthday, 10 March. The first thing he did when he was born was to pee all over me, and I said, 'You can pee on me whenever you like.' He loves to remind me of this. He's my beautiful blue-eyed boy."

DIANA THATER (artist, Los Angeles) "In 2004 I did simultaneous solo exhibitions at two museums in Germany, the Museum für Gegenwartskunst Siegen and the Kunsthalle Bremen. They were about three hours' drive apart, and I had a driver with a Mercedes to take me back and forth between the two as I installed both shows. I was addicted to the soundtrack from *West Side Story* at the time. They're still the best shows I've ever done."

ANNA CALVI (singer-songwriter, London) "In summer 2004 I was first introduced to the music of Kate Bush, and I listened to *Hounds of Love* incessantly. I was obsessed with wearing long, beaded necklaces."

ANNABELLE SELLDORF (architect, New York) "I had designed a cabin in Nova Scotia for my friends Robert Gober and Donald Moffett on a peninsula that can only be accessed by boat during the summer months. The logistics of building this little off-grid house with the help of the local lobster fishermen was a lot of fun. It entailed a lot of driving along the beautiful coast of Nova Scotia with my business partner, Sara Lopergolo, listening to Cat Power. I love that kind of driving."

LIZ COLLINS (photographer, London) "In 2004 I took a two-month break from work and travelled to India on my own. I studied yoga at dawn and dusk and volunteered in a dog rescue centre in between. Back in England, I got my own dog, Frinkle, the border terrier who changed my world."

NAOMI ALDERMAN (writer, London) "I was working part-time at the children's charity Barnardo's while I finished my first novel, *Disobedience*. I was convinced it was going to be a *terrible* book and that any publisher who saw it would just laugh hysterically.

I'd also just heard about this new online game, Perplex City, that was looking for a writer, and was trying to persuade them to employ me. Both things turned out well in the end."

CHARLOTTE COTTON (curator, Los Angeles) "Seven years after a failed marriage, I decided to make 2004 the year of change. I left the interesting but achingly mapped-out job I'd had since university, had an affair with a man who was different from anyone I'd ever met, and found a way to move to America, where I've spent most of my time since."

SIMONE ROCHA (designer, London) "I was 17, living just outside Dublin. I think I spent most of that year hanging out in a field smoking with boys, like all good teenagers."

What were you doing 10 years ago?

DANIELLE STEEL (writer, San Francisco and Paris) "Ten years ago as I write this, I was on a boat in Italy with my five youngest children and their friends for our annual summer holiday. They were in their teens then, and we were probably in Sardinia, Corsica or Portofino, fishing and swimming every day and laughing a lot. Those annual summer holidays on boats we chartered are some of their happiest memories, and surely mine."

MARINA O'LOUGHLIN (restaurant critic, London) "I'd been reviewing for the London free sheet *Metro* for four years, and both *Metro* and I had grown into our roles. The paper had turned into a roaring success, its contributors being taken seriously for the first time. In 2004, Corbin & King launched the Wolseley, a restaurant that took London by storm, packed every night with everyone from Lucian Freud to Bryan Ferry. Full of my new self-importance, I swanned in. I still got the worst seat in the house."

HONEY DIJON (DJ and music producer, New York) "I was spending a lot of time in Paris, DJing at underground clubs such as Gibus and Redlight — Paris had a very rich and vibrant nightlife back then. I was also dating a very sweet young Frenchman named Michel. His family owned a stable where he came from in the north of France. It was the first time I ever went horseback riding. Michel and I parted ways in 2007; he now lives in Williamsburg, like most French expats."

MARY FAGOT (creative director, Los Angeles) "One minute I was on a video set for a rapper named Chingy, with coloured vinyl and lights and bumpers and an absolutely gigantic chrome ball that was meant to look like we were shooting inside a blinged-out pinball machine. Then I was in New York, developing projects with artists like Fischerspooner and OK Go, and really finally starting to figure out where I fit in the world. Everything was just taking off. It's been quite a decade since!"

CLEO ROCOS (entertainer, London) "In September 2004 I went to Andalusia to train as a matador. Over five days, I did a crash course in the techniques of bullfighting and was thrust into a bullring to face a bull on my own. The bull rammed into my thighs and pelvis, leaving me with a scar on my hip bone, but I managed to remain on my feet until I got some clear passes with the cape. Without doubt, one of the most exhilarating experiences of my life."

ALICE RAWSTHORN (design critic, London) "Some of the things I enjoyed 10 years ago: Quentin Tarantino's *Kill Bill: Volume 2*, reading Colm Tóibín's *The Master* and Peter Ackroyd's *The Lambs of London*, and wearing a 1940s-style red crêpe Marc Jacobs dress that I still love today."

CHRISTIANE AMANPOUR (broadcaster, London) "I was in Iraq and got a world exclusive by getting into the Baghdad courtroom where Saddam Hussein was brought for his first appearance since being captured after the US invasion. It was electrifying, as no one in the world had seen or heard from him for a year. I heard him before I saw him, as he shuffled in with his clanking chains around his feet and hands. Everyone thought justice for this brutal dictator would be the start of a bright future for Iraq. It wasn't."

3.

Give in to your big-hearted instincts and reap the rewards — you will never tire of the joy of abundance.

Gener-
osity

of
spirit

Hosting

Parties should be fun — not just for the guests but also for the host. That means preparation is paramount. Serious forethought delivers an event that runs on its own joyful momentum, allowing the party-giver to join in the dancing instead of hanging up the coats and pouring the drinks. The finer points of the peerless welcome are considered here.

By Emily King

There's little that beats basking in the triumphant aftermath of throwing a great party or hosting an especially entertaining dinner. The feeling of being pleasantly spent, in tandem with a flood of thank-you messages and the relief that it's over, makes for utter bliss. After my wedding, on a New Year's Eve more than 20 years ago, and over a hefty breakfast, I remember relishing stories of guests going home in unlikely couples. Similar satisfaction followed a December celebration a few years later that began with fish pie for 30 and ended with our friend Cerith turning himself into a living, dancing Christmas tree by borrowing all the baubles from the pine I'd dressed days before. Then there was the party in Venice where dance-floor abandonment was followed by dockside heroics: in my slightly mangled memory, someone acted as a human bridge over which euphoric guests scrambled onto the last boat home. Even a gentle supper with friends can generate a pleasant buzz in the mind as you empty the dishwasher the next day.

But whatever the rewards, parties are stressful. Assembling people and entertaining them are integral to the course of an ordinary life: from the teenage birthday party or student back-to-mine through to the dressed-up 50th, these gatherings stake out our most significant moments. Yet for most of us they still stand apart from the normal run of things. The smallest event — feeding a couple of people on a week night, for example — has the power to divide my existence in two, with a mild sense of anxiety blocking my view of life beyond my guests' arrival.

Part of the problem is that we're living not in an Emily Post etiquette society but rather a post-etiquette one where the old rules no longer apply. For the most part, that's a good thing — alternate-gender seating, now on the decline, should have disappeared years ago. But it does mean party-givers have to imagine events into existence pretty much from scratch, and the onus is now on guests to be thoughtful in unprescribed ways. One 1950s etiquette book advises guests to send flowers several hours in advance of a party so the hosts won't be tangled in stems when they're busy with other things. I love being handed flowers as a guest arrives even if it renders me momentarily paralysed between wilting tulips and a tray of burning bruschetta, but there's something charming about the degree of consideration the instruction implies.

What's needed is a broad set of principles to get us through all tomorrow's parties. How can we achieve the perfect balance and create an event that seems appropriately celebratory without becoming a martyr, a monster or a hopeless drunken mess? According to my friend Paola, it's all about *sprezzatura* — the appearance of ease disguising the expenditure of effort (Paola has said quality in spades). The idea is to give guests a sense of occasion and make them feel looked after, but not to the extent that they're unable to relax or that they start to fear for the sanity of the host. BYOB parties work best when there's someone on hand to receive bottles and put them in the fridge. A butlered affair is very nice, as long as you feel cosseted rather than policed.

The problem with setting out principles, of course, is that counter-examples always emerge. Disguising the struggle seems the best advice, and then I remember my friend Angus, who flusters his way through enormous dinner parties yet is a marvellous host. He never sits down once throughout the evening, but he radiates an enormous sense of enjoyment. Endeavour can be very touching.

A couple of years ago, I wrote a profile of the entrepreneur and British peer Martha Lane Fox. When I interviewed her friends, a number of them noted what a fantastic host she was, so I solicited her advice for this piece. "It's never about the hostess and always about the guests," was all she would say. Implicit in her answer is a relishing of the process. The author of *The Three Musketeers*, Alexandre Dumas, devoted several pages of his memoirs to a ball he threw in Paris during the 1833 carnival. Having taken care of the decoration by asking his artist friends, including Eugène Delacroix, to paint the rooms, he turned to the question of supper. "I thought of providing the main foundation of this with game killed by my own hand; this would be both a pleasure and an economy," he wrote, and he and his companions duly shot nine roebuck and three hares. During the party, he received 700 guests and served them 300 bottles of Bordeaux, 300 bottles of burgundy and 500 bottles of champagne. "Wonderful to relate that there was enough for everybody to eat and to drink!" I doubt Martha wields a gun, but her reputation suggests she has the same expansiveness of spirit.

Away from the glamour of 19th-century excess, the reality is that throwing a party requires attention to a number of dull details some days in advance. There needs to be a place for people to leave coats and bags; it's best if they can get food and drink easily without creating bottlenecks; there should be some kind of system for stashing used plates and glasses, and so forth. If the party is at home, the most practical approach is to envisage what's likely to come to pass — even do a walk-through — and then prepare for it. Similarly, if you want your guests to be drinking champagne at 8 p.m., eating at 9 p.m. and dancing two hours later, tell them so on the invitation. People are much more likely to cooperate if they have been warned. Whatever your hopes, though, be prepared for something completely different to take place. Among the few light moments in Lars von Trier's gloriously gloomy *Melancholia* is the thwarting of the wedding planner, played by the terrifying Udo Kier, as the assembled guests destroy his carefully rehearsed programme with drunkenness.

Margot Henderson, London caterer extraordinaire and author of the cookbook *You're All Invited*, knows one secret to a good party. She believes in the power of a well-thought-out dinner placement — giving people the reassurance of knowing where to go while adding the spark of unlikely juxtapositions. When I recorded an interview with Margot on the subject, the sociable young woman who transcribed it misheard "placement" as "plus one", which is almost the opposite, though I see the virtue of both. Bringing uninvited company to a seated dinner is obviously a no-no, but a well-chosen extra at any other kind of party can be very welcome. Parties are celebrations of life thus far, but they also mark or even create new turns, and to that end, fresh acquaintances are no bad thing.

Under no circumstances should parties be employed as public demonstrations of the respective importance of your various friends, though. Having been on both sides of the invited-after-dinner experience — as a part of the invaded inner circle and as a member of the intruding horde — I have a particular aversion to two-tier hosting. A good party is an all-in-it-together experience.

One of Margot's other tips is to create the appearance of abundance: a mass of shiny glasses, a pile of loaves of bread, a pyramid of Eccles cakes. Beyond the look of plenty, it's wise to be as generous as you can be. Everyone responds well to large quantities of nice food and drink. That said, there's no need to be a slave to your guests' every preference. Attending parties orchestrated by Margot, I've always been struck by her authoritative provision of a small repertoire of delectable dishes.

I'm no expert host by any means, but I have three children, an extended family and a moderate sense of occasion. These are my core tips, gathered over the years. Food and drink: unless you have very peculiar tastes or dietary restrictions, serve what you, the host, like to eat and drink best. I had a particularly delicious ginger cake at a recent 50th birthday party, and our host's delight at our enjoyment of his favourite food was particularly charming. Decoration: good lighting is essential; everything else is an extra. Cleanliness: if you're having your party at home, don't freak out. It won't look nearly as disgusting to other people, but maybe pay a little attention to the corner where you feed the cat. Staff: if you can muster the resources, even the smallest party can benefit from someone doling out drink and rounding up used glasses. And last: accept a degree of anxiety. There's nothing wrong in outsourcing what you're able to — the cooking, the serving, the cleaning — but if you farm out the desire to please your guests, and with it the little twinge of apprehension it's likely to engender, then you've probably missed the point.

Magnum

By Seb Emina

A bottle of wine is 750ml. That's probably for the best, isn't it? Five or six glasses is a perfect quota for civilised meals, or usefully frank tête-à-têtes, or cathartic nights alone on the sofa, these being the three main purposes of wine. And a standard bottle is simple to store and straightforward to brandish in the face of a party host to signal that we are good and thoughtful people.

The trouble is, said host often acknowledges the bottle with a vague smile and places it absent-mindedly in the bureaucratic limbo that is "on the side for later". A better way to make a splash with your vinous contribution is to do something unexpected, something theatrical. Don't bring a regular bottle. Bring a magnum. Immediately you are 1.5 litres generous — twice as much so as the normal party guest. And you will get the party started without so much as opening it: a magnum — so rare, so large, so ostentatious — is an instant conversation topic.

But there's more to a magnum than volume and spectacle. Any expert will tell you that when the ageing process takes place in a "mag", as they're affectionately termed, the wine that eventually comes out has a more vivid flavour. Bigger bottles offer "a better and deeper taste," says Francesco Previtera, a sommelier I met at a wine tasting on the Aeolian island of Salina. "The more wine that's inside, the better the mix of all wine elements: more molecules, more scent elements, more flavour components." And a greater quantity of liquid results in a larger wine-to-air ratio, a slower maturation process and consequent improvements in what the unscientific masses might term "deliciousness". Reds, whites and champagnes are all potentially enhanced by magnum ageing (though the average domestic fridge may struggle with the latter two).

Indeed, when a magnum of a certain vintage is available, it's a sign that its maker felt it worthy of such elevated treatment. "Usually when you find a wine in the bigger bottle, you can be sure that it's a great wine chosen by the producer to be bottled in a larger vessel," Previtera says. In recent years magnums have started popping up in wine shops and restaurants with increasing frequency but their presence is still a somewhat reliable guarantor of quality, and they remain rare enough to give off an aura of delightful occasion.

Opening a magnum can be a heroic act. Occasionally, if the opener is short and the table tall, an elevating platform such as a chair will come into play (avoid this if other magnums have already been opened and consumed). Standing the bottle upright for a day beforehand will allow any sediment to sink to the bottom. Decant, if possible. Pour carefully. A drip-free end to the process can be achieved with a gentle rotation of the bottle. A magnum contains between 10 and 12 glasses of wine, which is, let's be honest, more in line with the demands of many dinner tables than the somewhat spartan regular ration — and it saves us from the awkward hassle of gauging communal interest and then flagging down a waiter.

And when, after eight or nine outings, the magnum starts to feel like just another everyday bottle, there is the option of upsizing again. There are the jeroboam (three litres), the methuselah (six litres), the balthazar (12 litres) and the nebuchadnezzar (15 litres). Each is named after a biblical king, and each requires an increasingly wily solution to the challenge of extracting the liquid — merely holding the bottle and tipping it no longer being practical without a coordinated effort (some use surgical tubing to siphon the wine off, petrol-style). A "neb" contains the equivalent of 20 standard bottles. It will get the party started — and then it will get it finished again.

Excess

By Joan Juliet Buck

On assignment in Moscow a few years ago, I had dinner with my friend Owen in a restaurant jammed with bevelled glass screens and mahogany panels. The waiters were heavily costumed, and my handbag was given a miniature chair of its own. My first course was a mousse of smoked trout so delicate, so unusual that I had barely finished it before I asked the waiter, who looked like an extra in *Gigi*, to bring me the same thing again. Owen choked on his vodka. "That's so... excessive," he said.

My neural pathways lead to multitude. Any appealing object sets off a desire for other objects similar in genus, design and function, related by shape, pattern, colour, provenance. The string of associations that said object unleashes comprises everything I have ever seen, touched, eaten, drunk, borrowed, lost, found, given, been

given, bought, misplaced or read about. Anything can be Proust's madeleine: a linen towel, a cut-glass tumbler, a yellow rose, a pair of gloves, a duet in an opera, a tune playing on Spotify in a shop, a really good smoked trout mousse. Should that object be for sale, I'll spend money on assembling a family of associations.

"No instant collections!" yelped a French boyfriend at the flea market as I became mesmerised by dour architectural prints of late 19th-century yellow-brick factories. But the next booth had prints of sphinxes torn from a book about ancient Rome, and the associations they brought up — my grandmother's lamps, Oedipus, ancient Egypt, Jean Cocteau, winged women with animal lower halves — were richer than yellow-brick factories. I still have some sphinxes.

I'm wired for plenty. A London shrink once jokingly diagnosed it as horror vacui; at the time, he was talking about my penchant for what is now called polyandry. But I see the world as divided into the excessives, who suffer from that fear of empty space — generous types with volatile tempers who believe More Is More — and the measured, who appreciate midcentury modern, purge their wardrobes and serve you one lamb chop at dinner. Horror vacui causes agoraphobia in Bauhaus rooms, can lead to body fat and, if unchecked, ends in hoarding. Freud certainly had it; the photographs of his study at Berggasse 19 show far too many little Egyptian and Greek statues lined up on his desk. No surprise that he's the father of free association.

I am surrounded by herds of contradictory associations, each one an elated response to a flea market or a journey to an interesting place, and these collections do not speak to one another. Five articulated brass fish; an ice bucket and various plated bar articles from the 1940s, and I don't even drink; God knows how many Hopi rattles — those gourds painted white, decorated with primary colours and adorned with feathers. The rattles, however, have no business on a shelf next to the remaining sphinxes. Did I mention that the floors are Kilim rug on petit point on Soumak on Ourika? There's no order to my excess.

Excess is more useful for the rich, whose money allows them to focus, or at least have enough room to allocate different spaces to their associations. In Palm Beach, Florida, I know a house that's a series of open pavilions set in a palm garden. In one, filigree shades edged in beads throw shards of light onto damask cushions on striped banquettes in front of tiles painted with turquoise curlicues and tulips. That room is the Topkapi harem room. Moroccan rugs and lamps and pots and baskets and many ewers and brass camels are gathered in the tented room across the garden, where dinner is served. That's order within excess.

What do you give as a thank you?

In the first issue of The Gentlewoman in 2010, 39 of the magazine's favourite friends shared how they show their gratitude.

CLARE WAIGHT KELLER (designer, London) thinks of a person's interest, and then finds an art or photography book to go with it. For a friend who is very fond of horses, she sourced a book on horses by Kelly Klein, who readers will recognise as the ex-wife of Calvin.

KIRSTY WARK (broadcaster, Glasgow) has a shortlist of practical presents to draw upon when giving to her female friends. It comprises "fabulous stationery from Kate's Paperie in New York, a pack of Chanel eye masks, snowdrop bulbs and Wolford Velvet de Luxe tights in black."

GILLIAN WEARING (artist, London) is very pragmatic when she thinks of gifts for her husband, the artist Michael Landy, a man who once destroyed everything he owned. "I love buying him Marks & Spencer's jumpers," Gillian says. "Especially the cashmere ones as they are so classic and don't have labels sewn on the front of them or any other obtrusive feature. I usually buy myself one as well."

VICTOIRE DE CASTELLANE (designer of Dior Joaillerie, Paris) scours the auction website eBay to amass vintage gifts, especially the bucket bags and wooden box purses by the Texan designer Enid Collins from the late 1950s and 60s. "They are all unique and poetic and naïve," Victoire says.

DR DJURDJA BARTLETT (fashion historian, London) loves to give food. "My favourite shopping destination is the road that leads from the tiny village of Punta Križa on the island of Cres, off the Croatian coast, to the ferry that takes you to the mainland. There are many tiny food stalls from which the villagers sell the produce they grow and make themselves: lavender honey, hard sheep's milk cheese, smoked goat's cheese, olive oil and grappa infused with wild herbs." Last summer, Djurdja went one step further, making six jars of her own fig jam using fruit she collected on the island. "These presents cheer anybody up," she says.

KATE and LAURA MULLEAVY (designers of Rodarte, Pasadena) love to give old books with personal inscriptions. The sisters once gave their best friend Johnson "a book inscribed, 'dear peter pan, from alice in wonderland, Merrie Christmas, 1940'." They say that Caravan Books in Los Angeles is a good place to buy old Jack London, Jack Kerouac and Richard Brautigan books.

HOLLY BRUBACH (writer, Pittsburgh) gives "fabulous" Italian salt, Sale alle Erbe delle Marlunghe by Vignalta, as a hostess gift when she goes visiting. It is a blend of sea salt, fresh rosemary, fresh sage, fresh garlic and black pepper. "Rather than drying the herbs, they just mix them with the salt, which preserves them," Holly explains. "The label says this is an old tradition of the Veneto." Otherwise, for architects, designers and friends who hunt treasures in flea markets, Holly's "perfect" present is a leather-covered Hermès tape measure. Not only is it sleek and compact enough to fit in a bag or pocket, it measures in both centimetres and inches. "I like the idea of giving my friends things they wouldn't buy for themselves," she says.

PENNY MARTIN (editor, London) gives vests from Hanro of Switzerland, the seamless cotton ones with the satin-covered spaghetti straps.

STÉPHANIE COHEN (writer, Paris) relies on two favourite books as her failsafe presents: *Dalva* by Jim Harrison and *Aurélien* by Louis Aragon.

JANET STREET-PORTER (broadcaster, London) is opinionated about the art of present-giving. "There's too much promotion of buying," Janet says. "I give jam I've made, or chutney. I don't agree with constantly telling people to buy things or being held up as a style guru or expert."

Generosity of spirit

TAMMY KANE (co-director of Christopher Kane, London) recently went through a neon light phase. "A few of my close friends turned 30 this year so I commissioned neon lights with three- or four-letter words relating to their personalities. When they saw what they were, the smiles on their faces were priceless. To know that they are used in their homes or offices makes the gift really special."

LIZ COLLINS (photographer, London) buys something fantastic and luxurious from Louis Vuitton when she is looking for a special present for her girlfriends.

CLAUDIA SCHIFFER (model and actor, London) goes bespoke, commissioning jewellery for her friends that is either of unique design, directed by Claudia herself, or inscribed with special messages.

JOAN JULIET BUCK (writer and editor, Rhinebeck, New York) collects gifts for future dispersal when she travels: a pack of chewing gum called Delete and a phallic walnut-and-raisin sausage by Güllüoglu from Istanbul; *The Essential Mormon Cookbook* from Utah; nuggets of copper or a piece of chrysocolla from Arkansas; and slabs of dark chocolate with green chillies and dried cranberries from the Chocolate-Smith in Santa Fe. Joan also says that newlyweds get "a really good French garlic press."

LYNNE COX (swimmer and writer, Los Alamitos) relies on the rich breadth of rose varieties for her gifts, particularly for marriages and moments of success. "I find out what his or her favourite colour is," she says, "and tie the name of the rose to something I write on the card that I send along with it. For my friend who retired and has done so much with her life, I sent a rose called Gold Medal."

MARY FAGOT (creative director, Los Angeles) helps friends glam up by giving them glitter nail polish by Face Stockholm.

What do you give us a thank you?

VERONICA DITTING (creative director, London) has an ingenious solution for a thoughtful present. Recently, she asked 18 of a friend's nearest and dearest to guess his favourite song, then made their suggestions into a compilation CD.

GARANCE DORÉ (street photographer, Paris) books her friends a massage at the Espace France Asie in Paris, which she says offers seriously good Thai massages with exceptional deep-tissue pressure. The Espace is near Place de la Madeleine.

ZOE CASSAVETES (film director, Paris) says she is profligate with her gifts, giving them whenever she finds "the perfect gift for the perfect person". But Zoe particularly likes giving wine or champagne glasses: "They are a perfect thank-you gift as they always invoke the idea of a good time."

SUSAN IRVINE (writer, London) is bored with giving tasteful presents, although she is still happy to receive them herself. "When on the giving end of a gift," she says, "I like to offer Scottish novelties such as Kilted Mac-Gingers — boxes of gingerbread men wearing edible tartan kilts and sporrans — from Ashers Bakery in the Scottish Highlands. My other great favourite is the Instakilt, the beach towel that doubles as the sexy item of Celtic male attire."

SARAH MURRAY (casting agent, London) has the solution for a gift to give to the supremely wealthy: lord and lady titles. These titles can be passed down through the family, and give ownership of a usually tiny bit of land. "It's all very legal and you are allowed to change your names and status to Laird and Lady," Sarah says. "I must say it does go down really well when the recipient opens the ownership pack."

KITTY TRAVERS (CEO, La Grotta Ices, London) gives a present that she would like to receive and which she is hoping will be shared: a box of ravioli that is like sheets of stamps, from Camisa, either from its Old Compton Street store in London or from its online deli. She also loves to give a huge piece of Parmesan.

PRINCESS JULIA (nightclub legend, London) gives her friends a present that she can share: "two beautiful, unique glasses — tumblers or cocktail glasses, vintage or otherwise — and a bottle of bubbly or the favourite drink of the person I'm giving the present to."

EMILY KING (curator, London) has a fear of imposing stuff on people. She concedes that "one of the few things that improves every life is a really good bottle of olive oil." She particularly likes oils that smell of fresh-cut grass.

JINA KHAYYER (writer, South of France) acted the mischievous aunt when she gave her niece Darya a silver iPod filled with songs this past Christmas. Darya is 11, and while the iPod was loaded with radio-friendly songs like "Poker Face" by Lady Gaga and "Umbrella" by Rihanna, Jina also put on the playlist "Fuck You" by Lily Allen, which she says made Darya feel "totally grown up". Jina was helped by her friend Jean-Marie Delbes, DJ at Le Montana in Paris, who in the process discovered "Because of You" by Kelly Clarkson, which became his personal December 2009 hit.

RACHEL ATHERTON (champion downhill cyclist, Dyfi, Wales) believes in giving a gift that lasts a lifetime: a tree. Any kind, but she stipulates they must be ones you can have at your house. "I've yet to meet someone who can't appreciate a tree," Rachel says.

SARA PÉREZ (winemaker, Falset, Catalonia) heads to her cellars for a special magnum of one of her wines, a Clos Martinet from an old vintage like 1998 or 2000, for most gift occasions. But for a truly special present, Sara says, "I adore giving my personal soaps, made by my own hands from our own olive oil and aromatic plants, or natural inks for writing made from our grapes." As with her wines, "everything is organic, of course."

What do you give as a thank you?

SISSEL TOLAAS (artist and perfumer, Berlin) gives Guy No. 01, a fragrance she created based on male sweat. Sissel will not disclose the exact identity of the guy behind Guy No. 01, but will reveal that her full range of fragrances, which number 16 in total, are from "extremely excited men, collected at the moment of excitement". Giving one of these essences, Sissel says, "is like giving away someone's body. And I think that's a very generous gift."

JULIE VERHOEVEN (artist, London) gives a book that has proven so successful a gift that she has even made new friends when bonding over it. "My pressie of choice is *The Philosophy of Andy Warhol (From A to B and Back Again)*," Julie says. "It's a beautiful book and I like the idea of a pass-it-on paperback. You don't need to be a Warhol fan to appreciate it, but then, I would find it hard to have a friend who didn't appreciate him. It's a truly insightful book, very touching and, above all, funny and all-embracing. There is a real clarity in his views on life and loves and it has an iconic cover to boot."

INEZ VAN LAMSWEERDE (photographer, New York) heads to D. Porthault, the linen specialists, for its travel accessories and pouches for lingerie. "Everything is so precious and delicate and has that old-world feeling which I love," she says.

SARAH ANDELMAN (creative director, Paris and Chichester, New York) recommends giving notebooks from the house of Smythson, inscribed with phrases such as "Bright Ideas" or "Blah Blah Blah".

MO VELD (journalist, Amsterdam) was inspired by a gift her boyfriend gave her: a sterling silver Parker Sonnet Ciselé pen. If she could afford it, she'd love to hand them around to her girlfriends.

ROBYN (singer, Stockholm) suggests a handy and highly personal fall-back gift: vintage sunglasses.

CHARLOTTE COTTON (curator, Los Angeles) stockpiles turquoise tins of 20 gold sparklers from Fortnum & Mason, which she thinks cost £8.95. She buys in bulk because, she says, "I suspect someone else in the world has worked out that it's a genius gift and they can be out of stock at times."

VIVIANE SASSEN (photographer, Amsterdam) loves "giving a big silver spoon to newborn babies, with their name engraved in big Gothic letters."

ENIKÖ MIHALIK (model, New York) has two key passions with presents: wallets and chocolate. Last Christmas she bought wallets from Burberry for almost everyone she knows, while the year before they were from, variously, Gucci, Fendi and Prada, along with one from Louis Vuitton for herself. But she says chocolates are her particular speciality, and buys them from Godiva and Lindt.

MARIA BAIBAKOVA (curator, London) is a fan of giving teas from the Parisian tea house Mariage Frères. "Ruschka rooibos in particular," she declares, is a perfect blend for afternoon supping.

NATALIA VODIANOVA (model, Paris) advises: "I always give jewellery."

4.

How

The new challenge is not how to keep up with your friends but how to keep yourself apart and your life private.

to be...

Alone

Once, all it took to protect a woman's creative privacy was a room of one's own. A century on, something else is required: permission to retreat.

By Susan Irvine

As the world went into lockdown in the spring of 2020, *The Paris Review* ran a series of interviews from its archives that seemed to shed light on our new reality. One was with Marilynne Robinson, the author of *Housekeeping* and *Gilead*.

Interviewer: When you were little, what did you think you would be when you grew up?

Robinson: Oh, a hermit?

This struck a chord. When I was 11, my mother pulled me aside. "Tracy's mother says you told Tracy that when you grow up you want to be a hermit. Is it true?"

It was true. But if it seemed peculiar then, how much odder would it seem to a mother now? For while the editors at *The Paris Review* were right in thinking that lockdown meant solitude, they were also wrong. We may have been physically separated in our private homes, but we were more connected than ever to the humming circuits of social media and the world wide web: Instagram, TikTok, Facebook, Twitter, email, internet, notifications. *Refresh. Refresh. Refresh.* What we call privacy is far less private than it was when I was an 11-year-old wannabe anchorite.

I never got to be a hermit when I grew up. But the desire for more hermitude (not a word, but it should be) has never gone away. When lockdown was announced I felt an illicit thrill: at last, permission to retreat, guilt-free. When all those lockdown poetry exchanges started up on email, the poem I always sent out was Yeats's "The Lake Isle of Innisfree" — "I will arise and go now, and go to Innisfree,/And a small cabin build there, of clay and wattles made;/Nine bean rows will I have there, a hive for the honeybee,/And live alone in the bee-loud glade."

I am no misanthrope, but at the end of the day I like to get into my rowboat and row across to the Lake Isle of Innisfree. For me, the phrase "no man is an island" is the stuff of nightmare.

There's only one rule of privacy, and that's refusal; your favourite word will have to become "no". Remember how marvellous it was to say that as a toddler? No. *No!* It's a verbal foot stamp. Emily Dickinson called it "the wildest word we consign to language." We need to reclaim that "no" if we are to revalue privacy.

Being a refusenik does not mean you dislike your friends and acquaintances. It simply allows you the privacy you require in order to refresh your desire to see them again. "No" can be said elegantly: "There is nothing I would have loved more than to be able to come to your book launch/supper party/show/baby shower. Sending wistful love from hermitude." In truth, you are not wistful about missing the baby shower; you are ecstatic, but there's no need to spill your guts here. Your essential tool in the etiquette of refusal is the past unreal conditional: "would have loved". The past unreal conditional is a wistful tense. It keens and beats its breast: *if only I could have come!* This is gratifying for the person you are refusing.

It's advisable to keep your reason for absence mysterious. If you don't feel bold enough to say you are "in hermitude", you can send wistful love from your own version of the Scottish wilderness. Perhaps because I am actually Scottish, people readily accept that I sometimes have to leave the metropolis to tramp across a withered bog, or gaze on stags or whatever "Scottish wilderness" gives rise to in their imaginations. Sometimes, I am in a Scottish wilderness IRL (or at least in Scotland). Other times, I'm wandering through a Scottish wilderness of the mind.

There are occasions when "no" cannot be said elegantly. Funerals. To these I say: go always. In general, you should never say no to a call from a broken heart. When a friend is dumped, be there. When a friend is having a girls' night / all-day picnic / book club event, head for the great bog of Cloone. Wistfully.

Next to the past unreal conditional, my favourite refusenik tool is the autoresponder. Email is one of the worst eroders of privacy, constantly compelling you into a ping-pong match of read and reply. The autoresponder replies for you. Job done. You *have* replied, even if only to say you will not be replying. People often set up autoresponders when they are on holiday. I do it any time I get email burnout. Sometimes I set it up to say "This inbox is only monitored on Fridays." Other times, "Throughout August I will be mostly offline." My most audacious autoresponder, posted in September last year, said, "I will have no access to email until mid-December and only sporadic access to mobile coverage. Looking forward to being back in touch on my return." Putting that out on my mail server, I felt like an animal that had chewed through the bars of its cage.

Decoupling from the overculture in this way can be baffling to others. And not everyone can get away with it to that extent. I can because I'm (mostly) self-employed. At the same time, being mostly self-employed means I have to come to people's minds as an option for any assignments. My radical strategy here is to use absence as my

---

USP. It's a highly specialist, high-risk niche in the modern career ecology. While everyone else is signalling that they are out there, my radio silence draws a kind of attention to me as busy elsewhere. That's the theory anyway.

Once I'm commissioned to do something, I have to turn up to meetings. I guess it doesn't look successful, it doesn't look popular, to be sitting with your hands in your lap while everyone else is thumbing their screens. I have got used to being in meetings where people are constantly interrupting themselves to tap rapidly on their phones or blurt, "I've got to take this", mobile already pressed to ear. Those people do look successful; they do look popular. Whereas I — phone on silent, notifications off for years — probably look as if drool is shortly going to trickle from my mouth. "I've just forwarded you the email," someone will say, and I'll reply that I'll see it when I get home then, because I don't do emails on my phone. This can rile them.

It's surprising how many people think I am enigmatic because I am not always available. "What are you *doing*?" is a question I often get when I shut down email for a bit. The real answer is mostly "Just the usual," but people find that hard to believe. I must be up to something if I've slipped behind a screen instead of being on one. (OK, sometimes I *am* up to something, but don't ask me what, it's private.) My other refusals are even more discombobulating. I haven't had a telly for two and a half decades, and while I do have a husband, I don't live with him. (I call this the ultimate in having your cake and eating it.) Someone I've known quite well for the past year only recently realised I had a husband at all. I don't seem to feel the compulsion to share at the contemporary frequency. My frequency of sharing is more the mental equivalent of the slow food movement. Slow sharing?

Although I seem the outlier, I sense a growing backlash against the constant pressure to be always sharing. It's assumed that the more connected we are, the better it is for our mental health. We share so much more of our private lives and inner thoughts than previous generations did. It's supposed to be a sign that we've evolved beyond those generations' hang-ups. There's an assumption that the unedited version of anything, including yourself, is always the more true.

I'd counter that assumption by picturing the mind as having an internal architecture, and considering the overly connected, oversharing one as the psyche's equivalent of what Rem Koolhaas called junkspace. "We have built more than all previous generations together, but somehow we do not register on the same scales. We do not leave pyramids," he wrote. No, what we leave, he says, are shopping malls, airports and giant theme parks: classic junkspaces. Junkspace, he continues, "is like being condemned to a perpetual Jacuzzi with millions of your best friends." This could equally well describe the mental spaces we inhabit.

Compare junkspace with the nooks explored in Gaston Bachelard's 1958 classic, *The Poetics of Space*. Even Bachelard's chapter titles make me feel good: "...The Significance of the Hut"; "Nests"; "Shells"; "Corners"; "Miniature"... Huts, nests, shells, corners — these are hermitages. Bachelard asks us to imagine living in a seashell and speaks about the "cottage chrysalis". No matter what my external habitation may be like, I want my internal habitat to be a cottage chrysalis. And when I talk about retreating into my shell, I don't mean as a fragile tortured soul who needs protection. I think of my shell as a miniature torqued palace of the mind. Instead of a shopping mall crammed with consumables, the shell-space is a volute of mother-of-pearl filled only with the sound of the sea. I think that's closer to the truth of who we are. The unedited self is the self that's actually harder to see under all the flotsam it's flailing about in.

Of course, there's plenty of junk in my head moving through at conveyor-belt speed; and yes, I spent 10 minutes on Instagram just now — #minishetty — checking out what Arnie Schwarzenegger's tiny pony, Whiskey, is up to. A bit of Whiskey never did anyone any harm. But too much would start to wear away my privacy of mind. Privacy is about editing what comes in as well as what goes out. Essentially, it is a desire for a kind of minimalism of mind.

To those who have tasted this mental minimalism for the first time during lockdowns and found that they liked it, I would say, don't be quick to relinquish your cottage chrysalis. Don't feel you have to let it go in order to thrive socially. Strangely, the opposite may be true. Absence makes the heart grow fonder, et cetera. But you will have to accept that some things will pass you by. Because just as there is only one rule of privacy, so there is only one enemy of privacy: FOMO. Let's be clear: if you are to enjoy privacy of mind, you will miss out on some stuff. You'll miss the stream of sweet jokes and banter along with the banalities and inanities that form the gossamer web of social media. Above all, you will miss out on the gossip.

But you'll gain inner space. Your very own Innis*free*. For me, this is the ne plus ultra of mental health: not feeling guilty because I'd rather spend the evening looking at cloud formations than "connecting".

I'll let Marilynne Robinson in that *Paris Review* interview have the last word. "I grew up with the confidence that the greatest privilege was to be alone and have all the time you wanted," she says. "That was the cream of existence."

Go, Marilynne, go. And shut the door behind you.

Anonymous

What does it take to remain anonymous in the 21st century? Is it even possible — or desirable? For those who want to try it out, delete social media accounts, always carry a wodge of cash and spend a life dodging the limelight.

By Marina O'Loughlin

In my tiny, rarefied world — that of newspaper restaurant critics — arguments on the subject of anonymity have raged ever since the role was formalised sometime during the 1950s. Whether or not anonymity is important or even necessary is hotly debated. I'm one of a dwindling anonymous bunch — there are no public photos; the photographic byline on my weekly newspaper column features me (well, not actually me) with my face covered by a large restaurant menu. Visually, no record of me exists.

I don't remember the exact moment I decided that anonymity was going to be my lot. But I do remember the reasoning. On the one hand, it was all loftiness and integrity — you can't report objectively on any institution that you're in bed with, be it food or art or politics. I believed that then and I believe it now. A restaurant might not be able to change intrinsically once a critic is recognised, but the experience most certainly will.

And on the other hand, I'm just not very sociable. Years ago, when psychographic tests were all the rage in the kind of primary-coloured ad agencies in which I used to work, my Myers-Briggs test results put me in solitary, in my own "silo". (About which my boss memorably asked the entire office, "Do we really need that silo?") And when I moved to London from a much smaller city, I loved the fact that nobody knew or cared who I was. I could behave how I liked — unsuitable liaisons, unfortunate wardrobe choices, unwise bouts of drunken country-and-western singing — without whispers or recriminations. I don't like parties, though in the early days I was naïvely thrilled to be invited to high-profile food-scene events. It didn't take me long to realise that when you have to pretend to be your friend's cousin from Up North, they're the dullest occasions imaginable — suddenly, nobody's interested in talking to you, sad but true. No, I enjoy being the cat who walks alone (with a plus one over the dinner table).

In this social media-infected age, where everyone is party to everyone else's absolutely everything, anonymity seems wilful, contrary. And it's downright tricky. How do you pay when a credit card bears your name, for example? What I thought was a wizard wheeze — paying with a card in my married name — crashed and burned when I idiotically agreed to a newspaper article about what the spouses of food people do for Valentine's Day. So now I find myself taking wads of cash around with me like a second-hand car dealer. And because websites demand an email address, I'm one of the few people who uses the telephone in this age of online booking — withholding my number so restaurants don't have a record of it. I do have a couple of online aliases, but I can never remember the passwords, or which one I've used. It's taken me a while, but I've finally learned to put my chosen alias beside each booking on my calendar. It seems simple in retrospect, but it took a lot of trial and error to get here.

All the subterfuge can venture into the bizarre, though. At one point, I started using my husband's phone number for bookings, but the savvier restaurants got wind of this and he was bemused to find himself whisked to the front of queues and given unbidden drinks when at business meetings over lunch. Many of the bigger establishments have cheat sheets — headshots of the major critics for spotting purposes — which I've occasionally caught sight of. I'm a silhouette. Which is fine. What's galling are the

---

accompanying bios: one of my colleagues was described as "tall and glamorous"; mine simply reads "tweets a lot".

There have been occasions when I've realised, with an encroaching prickly feeling, that I've been clocked. It mostly happens when a particularly beady publicist has managed to infer information about me from social media burblings: my accent, my friendship group, my predilection for a frosty martini. This results in what the — formerly anonymous — *New York* magazine critic, Adam Platt, described as "the strange, time-honored Kabuki dance that takes place between chefs and restaurateurs and the people whose job it is to cover them." They pretend they don't know who you are to pay lip service to the deception; you pretend you haven't noticed that they've noticed... Oh, it's a whole lot of fun for all the family.

But there's a more toxic subtext to anonymity these days: that of trolling and fake news. It is widely held that, psychologically, anonymity lessens the feeling of accountability. As someone who publishes but is also very active online, in a weird marriage of visibility and invisibility, I think my anonymity protects me from the anonymous. I believe I suffer less online abuse than some of my female peers simply because the trolls can't box me under "fuckable" or "unfuckable". In fact, there has been speculation that I'm a man, or a hive mind of several people — which is not, I feel, entirely flattering to my writing style.

By choosing anonymity, you also choose a degree of penury. It is hard to earn a decent living as an anonymous creative. Author or artist, fashion designer or performer, the loot usually pours in via personal appearances, whether in the flesh or — oh lucrative joy — a television profile.

There are, of course, exceptions: the singer Sia managed quite a few years before she unmasked. And Elena Ferrante's anonymity — more correctly pseudonymity — didn't curtail her bestselling career. She has eloquently outlined the reason for her decision: not wishing her work to be involved in the "circus of personality" of "the celebrity author", wanting it to be judged and read solely on its own terms. And when she was outed it was met with anger, outrage and accusations of sexism from the literary world.

I can see both sides, up to a point. And here's where I have to confess to having regularly worn another hat: I was for a long time also a travel writer for *BBC Good Food* magazine, a job that is impossible to do while anonymous. I had to meet people — for tours, for background information, for insight into the local scene impossible to glean from any amount of distant research. And when I packed my suitcase to leave the country, I left my cloak of anonymity behind.

It's remarkable to witness the difference between visiting somewhere as a known entity and slinking in unannounced: suddenly, the best tables were at my disposal, extra dishes would mysteriously arrive from the kitchen, a glass of champagne and delicious dessert wines bookending my meal. I don't care what my "out" colleagues protest — it's a lot harder to remain dispassionate when you've been showered with love. And then the worst bit: the chef, a look of pained anxiety on his or her face, issuing from behind the scenes to ask how everything was. In the pantheon of awkward social interactions, this one ranks close to the top. I would find myself turning into the little old ladies from *Fawlty Towers*. "Lovely! It was all lovely!"

Although there's something seductive about anonymity in these share-all times, gently, ever so gently, I'm making myself a tiny bit more visible. The irony that a lot of it is due to social media is not lost on me — Twitter, in particular, is an invaluable resource for insider recommendations when travelling and, if you're travelling alone, it's good to be able to meet those like-minded, helpful people for a drink. I even spoke on radio for the first time recently, something I'd always avoided out of fear that my accent might be a dead giveaway, as if I'm the only Scottish person ever to visit a restaurant. But if I were to give up anonymity completely, I'm not sure the benefits would outweigh the downsides. Even in seen-it-all London, I've eaten with famous critics and felt the atmosphere petrify as soon as they walked through the door. So, come out once and for all? I've learned to never say never, but I suspect I'll lurk in the shadows just a little bit longer.

Anonymous

Idle

A daily timetable of eight hours of work, eight of rest and eight of "what you will" may sound like an utopian ideal, but a century ago, it was a right worth fighting for. The will to do nothing is with us still — it's the means we seem to have lost.

By Ann Friedman

I spent the first half of last year immersed in writing a book. On the last day of June, my co-author, Aminatou Sow, and I pressed "send" on our draft, took our fingers off the keyboards and looked up from our screens. My shoulders ached from months hunched over my laptop. My mind was drained of verbs and adjectives. I had nothing else going on in my life. But all of that was about to change.

I had a 30-day window before our editors came back to us with their revisions. And I planned to spend that entire month doing nothing.

This is a well-accepted summer practice in many parts of Europe, but in the United States, where I live and work? It's absurd to take so many consecutive days of leisure. For many hourly-wage earners, a single one off is a rarity. I can't recall my own father, a small-business owner, ever taking more than a few days of holiday in a row. Even teachers, who have a long break built into the rhythm of their year, tend to spend those months off teaching at summer school or doing another job.

I thought of this break as a rare opportunity, but I did not think of idleness as valuable in and of itself. For most of my life, I've believed that "idleness" and "virtue" had no place in the same sentence. When I was in primary school, I would often begin my summer holidays by making a list. "Things To Do When I'm Bored." I collected rocks. I wrote 17-chapter short stories on a hulking, blue-screened IBM computer in my parents' basement. I recently found a *Baby-Sitters Club* calendar from when I was 10, filled in with activities like "play frisbee with Dana" and "go to the library". Modern childhood might be derided as overscheduled, but I was decades ahead of the curve.

My tendency to pack my schedule has only increased in adulthood. After seven years of self-employment, hard work has become my default mode. So how on earth did I think I was going to handle a full month of doing nothing?

Idleness is more than an empty space between periods of intense work. "Leisure is not the same as the absence of activity... or even as an inner quiet," the German philosopher Josef Pieper wrote in 1948. "It is rather like the stillness in the conversation of lovers, which is fed by their oneness." By that definition, I suspected I had never experienced leisure for more than a fleeting moment.

In my Midwestern household, cleanliness was a distant runner-up to hard work in the race for proximity to godliness. Even though my mother often says, "There's a lot to be said for leisure," the implication is that free time is valuable only because it is a break from one's normal state of dedicated labour. And it should not be spent in front of the television or asleep in bed: it should come with an agenda of its own.

And with the first draft of my book barely complete I was already asking myself, "What next?" Even though I was exhausted, I was overcome by a feeling of dread. I felt I should use this break as a professional-development retreat to figure out my post-book career move.

When I attempted to explain my conflicted feelings to my therapist, she asked if I was familiar with the "fertile void". I shook my head, thinking she must be referring to a self-help bestseller. No, she explained, the fertile void is a concept that originates in Gestalt psychotherapy and describes a period that occurs when something big has been accomplished after hard work or struggle. With this achievement in your rear view, you find yourself both ready to rest... and profoundly unsettled. It's a void, she said, because there is no force propelling you forwards or backwards, or anywhere. But — and this is where the fertile part comes in — this absence holds potential. If you don't pause, my therapist counselled, you don't experience the full benefits of that work. The space is where you intellectually and emotionally refuel.

This is not a new idea. Since the Middle Ages, farmers have been practising crop rotation, letting a field lie fallow for a season to replenish the nutrients in the soil before replanting it. Still, it was a revelation for me to hear relaxation being framed not as antithetical to work or progress but as necessary for it. The fertile void was the permission I needed to exhale.

In hindsight, I was primed to reconsider the value of idleness. Some months earlier, I had picked up *How to Do Nothing*, a manifesto by the artist Jenny Odell, and finished it in one go. Odell's book is a trenchant critique of the way constant digital access has allowed companies to monetise our every waking moment — prodding us either to produce or consume. My ingrained view of idleness as lazy rather than necessary is a hallmark of this modern era of round-the-clock work: Odell reminds us that a core value of the union movement was to limit the working week to 40 hours. In the wake of the Industrial Revolution, labour activists advocated for a daily schedule of "Eight hours for work, eight hours for rest and eight hours for what you will."

More than a century later, as labour protections have been eroded, so, too, have the hours for "what you will".

And during those precious hours, Odell argues that the only way to reclaim time from the digital abyss is to refocus on the minutiae of everyday moments. She "does nothing" by observing common birds of her native northern California and strolling in a rose garden near her home. Maybe, if you are addicted to lists and calendars like I am, you might actually need to schedule the "nothing", to practise the art of staying curious about the world by paying attention to it — completing your morning commute without listening to a podcast or a playlist created for you by an algorithm, say, or 15 minutes of phone-free meandering through your neighbourhood after dinner each night. This used to be how everybody lived. Now, for many of us, it is a way of being that must be learned and cultivated.

I did not, it must be said, enter the void easily. I set out to make it the *most* fertile void that had ever yawned open. In the notes app on my phone, I made a list of everything I would do while I was not working. I listed every single art museum in town. I added "reorganise bathroom cabinets", "complete a small quilt" (a belated wedding present), and a link to a list of items that should be included in an earthquake "go bag". (What, *you* don't relax with emergency preparedness?) I texted the friends I had neglected in my busiest pre-deadline weeks, professing that I was now free to get together any time. I decided I would roll out a yoga mat and stretch every morning, and bookmarked a video for this purpose that was enthusiastically titled *Rainbow Yoga! Yoga for All Ages! Yoga with Adriene!* None of these activities was technically work-related, so I told myself I would still reap the benefits of the void. I was just doing it *my* way.

It turns out that my way did not actually work. I did not meditate for hours to calm my mind. I did not fill pages and pages of my journal in a release of pent-up emotions. *Rainbow Yoga! Yoga for All!* was apparently mislabelled. I picked up novels and put them down again if they didn't hold my interest. I lingered in bed on weekdays and re-watched episodes of *RuPaul's Drag Race* from 2014. But I did have two-hour lunch dates with friends who live near-by, and engaged in long volleys of text messages with those who don't. I did a few stitches on that quilt. I took walks.

A few weeks in, I realised that what I was doing looked suspiciously similar to what I do in idle periods of my normal working life. I was simply expanding those moments of pointless relaxation so they bled into each other. "How we spend our days is, of course, how we spend our lives," the writer Annie Dillard once observed. And how we spend our precious few moments of leisure is, of course, how we will spend a full period of idleness.

I got more comfortable with the idea of idleness as the days ticked by. I still thought about my work every day. I fought the urge to tend to my inbox. I wondered about my next steps. But I wasn't tempted to act on anything. Every time I didn't open my laptop, I felt as if I were at sea on a luxury yacht, sipping champagne next to Rihanna. I was rich.

Indeed, what a luxury it was! Idleness, like a leather handbag so understated it *must* be expensive, whispers, "I've made it." It is perhaps the best reward for a job well done: permission to pause before beginning the next one.

This is easier for some than others. While men of a certain class have licence to enjoy a well-earned (and well-compensated) break without compromising their ability to be taken seriously, even the temporarily idle woman risks being perceived as a *Real Housewives* type, stirring up pointless drama and over-examining her every pore and wrinkle. In those countries that are inching towards gender parity in many areas of public life, women perform more uncompensated labour than their male peers, leaving precious little time for idleness. Historically, wealthy men have made great work not because they have better ideas but because they have more time to explore them; because they have benefited from the psychological space created for them by everyone else. This is space that women must create for ourselves. For us, idleness will not simply *occur*.

And what I have learned is that there will always be unread emails, unchecked items on the to-do list, unreturned phone calls, non-negotiable social obligations. Like time itself, forces of busyness are unceasing. The goal is not to work until there are no such demands and then enjoy a well-earned rest. Idleness must be added to the to-do list, etched into the diary. It must be valued and prioritised in such a way that a year is considered a disappointment if it has passed without a period of doing nothing, or an achievement is considered incomplete if it is not followed by at least the briefest of voids.

Fearless

By Susan Irvine

The French have an expression for twilight: *entre chien et loup*. By day we are domesticated like the dog. But at night, if we're lucky, a shaggy pelt peeps out from under our coats; lady into wolf. This is what I'm after as I set off at midnight.

Time to take a walk.

I'm not fearful on night walks, but I'm not fearless. I need a jolt of the stuff from time to time, like a shot of whisky burning all the way down. Just enough to give me a mindfulness I never have on the street during the day. It's not very Zen, this mindfulness, not very yoga. At 3 a.m. I wrestle with the urge to turn and see who is walking behind me. If I can get a look at them, I can sense them: OK, or scarper? But turning round is flinching. Like starting to run, it makes me prey.

I like an edge, but I don't seek danger. Not my definition of it, anyway. Some areas of the city I live in are never really deserted. Here in London, you can do night walking lite. You cross late revellers, early morning cleaners, buses lit up like ships in sea lanes. Other zones are forsaken. Westminster is my favourite of these, eerie and out of time. If anyone were to appear under its flickering gas lamps they would be in top hat and cape.

As I walk, my ears are pricked. Each sound is isolated, slightly askew. Even my own heels ringing on the pavement.

They don't sound... normal. Smells flare as if lit up. Beer, piss, woodsmoke from a barge, jasmine from a garden, then a greasy reek as someone exits Chicken Cottage.

You would think it's because you can't see well at night that the other senses are heightened. But it's not that. In a way, you see better at night. Eyes in the back of your head. And it's only now that certain things stand out in the city's architecture. Buildings unnoticed during the day come to the fore as if unveiled by the dark. Maybe it's the lack of distractions from people and traffic. Or maybe it's because the dark defamiliarises. The Russian formalists thought this was how literature worked. They thought that making an everyday thing seem strange allowed you to see it more clearly. "Art exists... to make the stone *stony*," Viktor Shklovsky wrote. But there's nothing like night to make the stones stony.

Being alone sharpens everything. I like to climb over the railings of residential squares and stand shoeless in black grass. I look up at the yellow warmth of windows and see people moving about like fish in glass tanks. I feel more real like this.

But sometimes it's good to bring someone else. In my case, someone who likes to plunge into back alleys more than I do, who's not afraid to follow drumbeats through an industrial estate to see if it's a voodoo ceremony or just an unofficial club.

We might scramble down to the foreshore of the river and listen to the tide. A seagull might fly by in the darkness. A voice from the street above might call "Night," and another answer "Goodnight," and the words seem cut out of the sky with diamond drills. We sit on the shingle for a while sharing a cigarette as the city sleeps.

Good

5.

relations

To be a guest or a godparent you need to be singularly selfless, thoughtful and considerate. Those same qualities will help you to celebrate well, too.

The birthday

The coming of age need not mean the end of an era — unless you want it to. Throwing your own celebration demands largesse, realism and the best catering money can buy. Get it right and you might find out exactly who you are.

By Sophie Hastings

Inspired by Evelyn Waugh's darkly satirical novel in which the Bright Young Things party their hearts out in 1920s Mayfair, the dress code for my 27th birthday party was *Vile Bodies*. Like the book, this particular birthday signified the end of an era. My father had died; our Norfolk home, the family HQ for three generations, was to be sold; and what my rudderless future held was anyone's guess. Cue class A drugs in every bathroom, Gatsbyesque quantities of champagne and 60 friends in strange and magnificent costumes dancing on the lawn till dawn. This was the 1990s, and it was by far the most debauched party I have ever given, verging on the nihilistic — a way of processing loss and fixing a moment in time.

Birthdays and how we observe them are far more complex than we admit, and there is a collective denial in our cultural insistence on exuberant celebration without much reflection, always looking forwards, never back. "Happy Birthday" is an onerous imperative, exerting even more pressure than "Merry Christmas" or "Happy New Year", with the onus firmly on the individual. We forget that not everyone enjoys the spotlight, whether it's that moment in the office when silence falls and then fills with excruciating small talk while everyone nibbles birthday cake, or dinner out and the sudden appearance of an attention-grabbing dessert you didn't order.

But not celebrating our birthdays — landmark ones especially — can leave us, as Nigella Lawson, who on turning 60 wrote in *The Sunday Times*, "feeling rather subdued as the day goes past unmarked." Escaping on holiday to spend the day with your head in the sand is not the way forward; you will only resent the hotel staff and the other guests, at least one of whom will be enjoying an ostentatious celebration of their own. Nor should you try to take your mind off your birthday by filling it with mundane tasks. Making a nine-hour round trip to collect a child from university, doing housework (unless in preparation for a party) or box-set bingeing with a family pack of Minstrels will lead to intrusive thoughts such as "Am I a complete loser?" Clothes shopping, exercise and complementary therapies are all fine, but they should be preambles, not the endgame. Hideous though the term "self-care" may be, there is something in it. In asking others to notice our birthdays, we acknowledge our place in the world.

It is incumbent upon us as feminists to do so. In ancient Rome, the first civilisation to celebrate the birthdays of ordinary people — it was pharaohs and deities before that — "people" meant men. Astonishingly, women's birthdays were not celebrated until the 12th century. So marking a birthday is our civic duty, like voting. The question is, how? It is wise to take stock before making plans. A birthday celebration is a signifier of who we are or who we want to be, and this differs with age. An 18th or 21st is a step in our progression to maturity, and birthdays are a chance to play at adulthood, so the glamour quotient should be high. The following decade is one of self-discovery, self-doubt and, ideally, a better understanding of where we're headed. Each passing year feels markedly different, so at 23, the dream birthday might be a festival in Croatia; at 26, cocktails and clubbing; at 29, an Ottolenghi picnic. Or none of the above: candles, plonk and a few good mates will do the trick.

With those pesky 20s out of the way, 30 should be a ball. Just three years on from my Norfolk bacchanal, I was living in Paris with my fiancé and five-year-old stepdaughter. There was a lot to celebrate, tribes to introduce and an apartment big enough for a party. As the Eurostar disgorged my friends and family, I knew that this weekend would leave us with a snapshot of a significant juncture. I'd grown up with many of these people, and we were entering our 30s together.

It's worth bearing in mind that, while some manage ageing better than others, we are not doing it alone. A single friend was so appalled by the advent of her fifth decade, she decided that she didn't want anyone to know where she was or what she was doing. But on the day itself, she was hurt and baffled that friends weren't lining up outside her door with croissants and champagne and wished she'd been a bit braver.

She was right about one thing, though — ageism is an issue. Once you tell people how old you are, there's no changing it, and you can't stop them totting up the years. Someone's age is never what's interesting about them, though; their attitude to life is what counts. And it's the birthday itself, not the age, that matters. Two friends I know are turning 47 and 50 this year and have decided to throw a joint 49th in Ibiza. Saying goodbye to a decade is just as important as ushering in the next. Acts of mutual celebration and commiseration are about authentic, shared grief and joy. On which note, I highly recommend the fuck-it 50s.

If you are not profoundly affected by reaching your half-century, you are either supremely well adjusted or in deep denial. For most of us, turning 50 evokes a combination of terror and incredulity, sadness at letting go of unfulfilled ambitions, relief at that unburdening and excitement at potential new adventures. While the Romans celebrated this seismic year with an unenviable-sounding cake of wheat flour, olive oil, honey and grated cheese, we tend to let our hair down with panache. With better food and better wine — and the fact that we no longer care what anyone else thinks of us — 50th birthdays are the best yet.

When you're the host, integrating the different areas of your life and combining diverse groups of friends, not to mention family, can be fraught, especially if you've spent decades trying to keep them at arm's length from each other. But it can work. Taking care of introverts and those who simply don't know anyone is vital, so make sure they are introduced to as many people as possible as soon as they arrive. Generosity of spirit loosens everyone up, as does fabulous catering; what you're after is a feeling of largesse.

The idea of throwing yourself a party, especially if you are single, might feel uncomfortable, even self-congratulatory. In which case, what to do? First, remind yourself that a party is a celebration of friendship, a way of telling people they are valued, not a "look at me" moment. But if shyness prevails, either join forces with a friend or ask someone to host it for you, making sure they know your preferences. Of course, you don't have to have a party at all. With a few close friends, the small but exquisite option can feel like perfection: mint juleps and petit fours at a gorgeous tearoom, a night at the opera, a luxurious dinner at home with lots of help in the kitchen. An added bonus with an intimate celebration is the likelihood of presents. At parties, gifts are often replaced with a decent bottle and anyway tend to peter out as we get older; cosy birthday gatherings, though, encourage thoughtful present-giving.

It is never too late to learn to celebrate. My next-door neighbour grew up in a family of Jehovah's Witnesses where birthdays were never celebrated. As an adult, she realised she wanted to acknowledge hers, but with no expectations or experience of birthday planning, it has taken time to find out what feels right. Starting at work, she brought in a cake one year, champagne the next. She intends to mask her 50th with a housewarming.

Under-the-radar celebrations are popular with reserved but determined party-givers and are useful gateways to the more straightforward approach, where you announce your continued existence with as much fanfare as you damn well please. I do think it gets easier with age: knowing when to break the rules, throwing caution to the wind in just the right way, is the sign of an evolved adult. A friend's mother, now 80, funded a joint 18th, 21st and 23rd for her three oldest children by selling the family car. While you may not have to go quite to those lengths to learn that birthdays are all about love and friendship, I'm hoping that, this year, we are more likely than ever to sing "Happy Birthday to Me".

Guesting

It's not just a matter of turning up at the right time on the right day — though that's important too. Being a good guest requires strategy, flexibility, amenability and some excellent gifts.

By Caroline Roux

"You really must come and stay" are some of the loveliest words in the English language, especially when pronounced by the owner of a 50-foot yacht or an artfully dilapidated shack on the coast of Costa Rica. "They've invited me to the boat/beach!" you whisper down the phone to your nearest and dearest, though no one else is listening, in a tone that's intended to be warm, low and discreet and is in reality the hysterical hiss of excitement tinged with triumph. You are going to be a guest! It is going to be heaven!

Well, maybe. But being a guest requires rather more than buying a ticket and packing a bag. There's planning and precision involved, whether the destination is a yacht, a country cottage, a city hotel or a caravan with pull-down beds, from the obvious (there's a pool: take a costume; there's no heating: take a sweater) to the more subtle ways to be happy in a strange place. Inflexible travellers might need to carry their own protein shakes/teabags/padded hangers if an absence of these will strain a good stay. A chronic workaholic might not be best advised to leave the Mac behind.

It doesn't do to overpack: no one wants to open the door to a person accompanied by an enormous suitcase; it implies a rather longer stay than discussed or a domestic takeover, however temporary. But it does do to anticipate the programme — boots for muddy walks; sand shoes for a coral beach; sundresses for sightseeing; a disco dazzler because, when it comes to it, you *will* end up at that club again. Borrowing items from a host should be a last resort, not a premeditated decision. (Only hats are exempt from this rule: cold-climate country houses and sun-drenched villas always seem to have plenty lying around for guest use. This might not apply in caravans.)

Of course, what a good guest requires most is an excellent host. "They don't get better than Iwan Wirth," an art-world acquaintance of the Swiss gallery owner says. "I've stayed at his place in Scotland, and I've never felt so comfortable. There's no sense of judgement, and there's loads of space. Meals are generous but completely calm and relaxed. He is the definition of gracious, and somehow that means everyone else behaves accordingly."

It's good to know that graciousness is contagious. But since the host sets the tone, the agenda and the menu, guesting might not be right for those with control issues, or food issues, or any other issues for that matter. A good guest "shall show neither annoyance nor disappointment — no matter what happens," the etiquette expert Emily Post declared in the early 1920s. Such old-world advice still prevails. The requirements for a 21st-century visitor have scarcely changed, with discretion, diplomacy and thought-fulness coming high on the list. "It's the ones who don't need much attention that I enjoy most. Not the ones who arrive in the kitchen at 9 a.m. and cling to your side for the rest of the day," says a regular host with a seaside home in north Wales. And the essential guest quality? Amenability. So best check your diplomacy and discretion levels before setting off, and if amenability isn't high on your agenda, perhaps check into a hotel instead (where some guests feel the act of payment voids the need for good behaviour).

There are some hosts, of course, who forget that host-ing demands a flexibility all its own. Last summer, a friend returned exhausted from a stay in a glorious Tuscan villa

---

where the increasingly irascible owner eventually decreed that arriving at the pool with the Wrong Type of Towel was a disinvitable offence. Another visitor to a different house party fell foul of a reputed social butterfly who is the best of guests herself yet turned out to be a major exponent of Altman's Privacy Regulation Theory in her own vacation space (this is when a person builds up undue stress by creating a disconnect between the actual lack of privacy they are undergoing and the extreme amount they perceive it to be). Imaginary emails summoned several guests home early. Regardless of these experiences, though, both visitors had the good manners to send handwritten notes of thanks. (No email, text or thinking/talking about it but not quite getting around to it will do.)

Not that guests are a blameless bunch. My recent run has been so unfortunate — one refused to get out of bed; another opened an expensive bottle of wine I had received as a gift — that all invitations are off. (Other annoyances: guests walking off with borrowed T-shirts, making liberal use of expensive face creams, unplugging the fridge to charge their phones, changing settings on computers, radios, televisions…) According to the pre-digital Mrs Post, "The guest no one invites a second time is the one who… 'dog ears' the books, leaves a cigarette on the edge of a table and burns a trench in its edge… who tracks muddy shoes into the house and leaves his room looking as though it had been through a cyclone." She still has a point, and I would suggest that using up all the hot water was as annoying a century ago as it is today.

But the most basic error a guest can make is to believe that an invitation to stay will save them money. What about the gift? It's essential: not a formality but a genuine token of appreciation. "I take a bottle of Armagnac and a box of Pierre Hermé chocolates from Paris when I arrive, and leave something more personal, like a beautiful book or scarf or a bowl, at the end of the stay," Julie de Libran, the exquisitely mannered French fashion designer, says. (The Armagnac is from her husband's estate in Gascony, the Château de Briat, and may come in a magnum-sized bottle. I would really recommend Julie as a guest.) "I like to bake something," says Rebecca Ward, a communications specialist and a marvellous host herself. "It shows you've taken into account the effort they've made for you."

Then there's the dinner that a guest should either offer to cook at home or pay for in a restaurant of the host's choosing. And filling up the car with petrol after a long journey. And, should there be any staff, leaving them a tip. Truth be told, being a guest can be expensive. I can attest to the fact that a couple of rounds of drinks in an upscale Monte Carlo bar (is there any other kind?) could pay for a couple of nights in an ordinary hotel.

The more I solicited advice on the art of being a guest, the more I heard the same. "The best guest is independent, calm, helpful and smokes outside," Julie de Libran says. "The worst takes personal things from your closets, moves your furniture and spoils something you love" (friend-ship included). Independence was highly valued, as was making the bed. "My favourite guests are the ones who know what they want," says the hotelier Catherine Butler, co-owner of At the Chapel in Bruton, Somerset. "I don't care if it's to go for long walks and read the paper or to be dead drunk by midday. The worst are the nervous ones that you don't know how to please." When Butler goes to London, she stays at the Dean Street Townhouse. "I like it because they've remembered me since my first visit. It feels like it's my place and I'm playing by my rules."

Indeed, if in doubt, perhaps it *is* best to head to the professionals. They love guests, for they are their very lifeblood. Take Guillaume Marly, who is savagely perfectionistic about the business of hospitality yet melts at the approach of a new arrival or a familiar face. "Guests need humanity," he coos, his Parisian inflection scarcely blemished by 30 years in the UK. "You must listen, watch, be gracious; you must make them look good." Marly, the managing director of the Hotel Café Royal in London, was the first managing director (it's what general managers are now called) of the wildly successful Chiltern Firehouse, the 26-room playground around which the hotel-meister André Balazs has kept celebrity London spinning since 2013. Before that, Marly worked at the Ritz, Claridge's and the Connaught (where he met Balazs — "André was an amazing guest; interesting and interested. The best kind").

Marly has seen it all in his time: the bloated celebrity demands, the hedonistic high jinks, the unsatisfiable, the insatiable. "There's an element of fantasy at a good hotel. And because all your requirements are continually met, that can do things to an ego," he says. "Strange things happen." His favourite guest is Gerry Parker, not a celebrity or an aristocrat but an old East End ruffian who uses Claridge's as a home from home. "He's a gangster, but a really charming old gangster," Marly says with a twinkle.

There is, I believe, such a thing as a professional guest, created by regular exposure to the highly sophisticated machine that is a top-class hotel. Light of luggage, canny about how to use the room service menu and the in-house laundry service, they see a hotel not as a "home from home" but more as a facsimile of domestic life without the hassles. "I lived in hotels for 10 years when I was single," Simon de Pury, the auctioneer and art dealer, once told me. "I've stayed in every room in Claridge's. And it was perfect for me. You simply don't have any worries about your living arrangements."

In the early to mid-1930s, Patrick Leigh Fermor walked, rode and cadged lifts from the Hook of Holland to Constantinople, staying along the way with a multitude of willing hosts, including an entomologist count in a Transylvanian castle and an Egyptian novelist in Athens. "Happiness, excitement, youth, good looks, eagerness to please and an open heart — Paddy had them all," says his biographer Artemis Cooper, explaining the British author's uncanny ability to find hospitality wherever he went, even on one trip at the Saint-Wandrille abbey in Normandy, which accommodated folk for free. All those qualities are still useful for today's guest, along with a seductively large bunch of flowers and an ability to not quite notice those awkward moments that inevitably pass from time to time between human beings sharing a space.

Postcard

By Sadie Stein

It is a particularly 21st-century phenomenon: emailing a person to ask for their postal address. In addition to removing any element of surprise, it also raises false hopes: should they anticipate a wedding invitation? A present? Well, no. What anyone I know can expect to receive, and with some regularity, is a postcard, be it a vintage oddity I can't resist picking up at car boot sales and charity shops, a piece of letterpress artistry, or actual proof of my infrequent travels. Most often, it is sent for no reason — just a quick hello out of the ether, tangible proof you're thinking of someone without the pressure or mechanism for them to respond.

I'm not alone. Myself and a number of friends around the country, and indeed the world, keep in touch almost exclusively via postcard. Granted, it keeps communication brief, but it leaves the recipient with a special keepsake to be treasured and one that, however economically, tells a story. Some of these correspondences date back to childhood, when we discovered the exciting autonomy and grown-up importance of letter writing. We'd send cards from family holidays to show off our well-travelled worldliness, not quite sure how to fill that small square of blank space with our careful handwriting. Later, as we moved apart, the flow of postcards kept relationships alive.

And then, of course, there's the aesthetics of the thing. With one friend I exchange sinister Victoriana; with another it's historic country houses. A globe-trotting pal and I have entertained each other for years with the adventures of a pair of fictional spinsters who communicate exclusively via vintage travel cards.

It's true that all my postcard correspondents are women. It seems that we all share a desire not just to disseminate information but to maintain a thread of shared sensibility, of deliberate civility, of thoughtfulness — a true luxury in this wired world.

God-parenting

An invitation to be a godparent can be the ticket to a magical lifelong relationship. But before accepting, find out precisely what's expected.

By Sophie Hastings

There are many ways to be a godparent. The richer, more influential or famously lovable you are, the more requests you are likely to receive, especially if you are childless. Either you accept every one and employ a PA to run the show or you think about each invitation very carefully and learn to say no, at the risk of offending your friends. Whatever your approach, successful godparenting is about time, empathy and imagination. These are the investments parents can hope for — and children will usually reciprocate, because friendships with adults who aren't family can be magical. Godparents open a window onto a world that is glimpsed but not yet experienced. Conversations in which the child is valued by a grown-up, with no emotional baggage attached, feed the soul, while excursions that take a child out of its daily life are small but significant rites of passage.

As the beneficiary of five godparents — two women and three men — I have always felt incredibly lucky, and their marvellousness is my pet subject. My father's cavalier departure from what the etiquette guide *Debrett's* claims is the "correct" cohort of three — two of the same sex as the child and one of the opposite — was, I imagine, simply because he wanted his friends in our lives. Whatever his motivation, he was right: five has proved the ideal number, and I have long regaled anyone prepared to listen with the joys of growing up surrounded by a constellation of kindly adults who have the patience to ask about your life, take you to the theatre and reflect their appreciation of your fascinating character with brilliantly conceived gifts.

My godfather James has always excelled at this. His presents were the highlight of every Christmas, large, extravagantly wrapped and usually delivered by chauffeur.

I never witnessed a delivery — they happened during the school day — but the description of a uniformed driver stepping out of a white Rolls-Royce and carrying my tinsel-covered present to our front door was intoxicating. And when I was 10, the best ever present arrived: a box full of Tottenham Hotspur treasures — tracksuit, shirt, scarf and posters. As a football-mad tomboy, I found that adults were often nonplussed by me, but with that present I was validated. Children — especially introverts — long to be "seen", and godparents are perfectly placed to do that.

There is, however, a wide divergence of opinion on the role of godparents in the 21st century, and some bafflement that they exist at all — especially if God isn't involved. The archaic significance of the role has been eroded: godparents don't tend to take responsibility for the children's spiritual instruction, nor are they (usually) signed up as potential guardians in the case of parental death. The consensus seems to be that godparents are a useful anachronism, good for presents and, possibly, internships.

And yet the parent-godparent-child triad can be life-enhancing for all concerned, and more relevant now than ever. It takes a village to raise a child, goes the adage, yet children are often brought up in small family units run by time-poor couples, many of whom will become insanely busy single parents. Whatever the set-up, there is no village to pick up the slack. Godparents are other adults who have agreed to love those children, to be there to celebrate their triumphs and commiserate their losses, and to listen to their worries without feeling they have to come up with a solution — something parents often do when all a child wants is simply to be heard.

But when my oldest son's godmother offered out of the blue to cover his school fees, we were taken aback. As a Chinese businesswoman educated in the UK, Pearl considers English private schools to be de rigueur and felt it her godmotherly duty to stump up the money. Thanking her for the stupendous offer, I demurred; Hector was happy at his primary school. Later, though, when he was miserable at his inner-city academy, Pearl paid for a Quaker school for two crucial years.

My younger son's artist godmother found the whole thing very odd. "You don't want to be financially beholden to someone outside the family," she said. "It's inappropriate." Was it? I wondered if Pearl had anticipated paying Hector's school fees. Did she think that's why we'd asked her to be his godmother? It hadn't occurred to me, but talking about it with friends, I encountered an opinion I hadn't heard before: that giving your child godparents was a form of gold-digging.

Certainly, *Debrett's* suggests that the contemporary godparent is there partly for financial reasons. "Godparents have been known to pay school fees, buy a round-the-world ticket... or even make a godchild their heir, if they have no other children," it reports. *Tatler* takes the same view, though its tone is more ominous: "If new parents ask you to be godparent to their precious little darling, they are lashing you, your money and your connections to them for life." Of course, few people can afford to subsidise other people's children, and *Debrett's* acknowledges that godparenting is, above all, about the relationship with the child: "Always let them know that they are in your thoughts," it advises.

We chose Pearl not for her money but because she is like a real-life fairy godmother. A pint-sized, couture-clad bombshell with a raucous laugh who has never wanted children of her own, she treats her godchildren like people worth knowing. She first took Hector and his sister, Tilly, out when they were five and three. After starting at Harrods' toy department, where they could pick whatever they liked, they had lunch at a nearby ice-cream parlour, where Hector dropped three top-heavy chocolate cones in a row and Pearl replaced every one. Back at her hotel, they discovered the joys of room service and the Cartoon Network. Now in their late teens, Hector and Tilly say nothing has eclipsed that day of epic wish fulfilment.

The artist godmother has so many godchildren she throws Christmas parties for them. But she also lets each one know they are held in mind, communicating on Instagram and — with the wild optimism of someone without children — by post. When Ludo wrote to thank her for a gift token, he enclosed a piece of art he'd made. She responded with a postcard, and he sent one back from his summer holiday. A written correspondence, with a teenage boy, in the digital age!

Parents must support these relationships and honour the only rule carved in stone: thank-you letters — or at least emails — are non-negotiable. My brother's decision one year to send a photocopied missive to each of his godparents after Christmas, filling in their names and the gifts they'd given, "to save time", rebounded badly. He received nothing from any of them the following year, or the year after. I was shocked by his rudeness, but perhaps he simply didn't know them well enough. I was close to my godparents, thanks to the fact that three of them lived in London and I saw them frequently; all five of his lived in the country and he rarely saw them at all. My friendship with James developed through visits to the ballet and opera — thrilling to me as a child — that led to decades of regular lunches. Now that he has retired to the countryside, I drive my dog to lunch with him in deepest Northamptonshire, a longish trip. But James always made time for me; now it's my turn.

It is virtually impossible to predict how seriously a godparent will take their role, so contingency is essential; appointing five means you're covered. I put this in place for each of my children, and from a group of 15, eight or nine stay in regular contact, with a couple more in the wings. Old friends tend to make committed godparents who are clearly in it for the long haul; some people get inexplicably spooked and disappear after the christening, while others gradually lose touch. Happily, the bolters are replaced by late bloomers who come good during the godchild's adolescence. Occasionally a godparent will fall out with the parents, and this almost always means the end of communication with the child. And there is the near certainty that at least one godparent will relocate. When I was eight, my godfather Dudley moved to LA to pursue his film career. We were close through proximity rather than effort on his part — he had been our lodger, was embedded in the fabric of my life — and I missed him. He didn't do letters, phone calls or godfatherly advice, but he always came to supper on visits to London, and he paid for me to fly out to stay with him one summer on Long Island — the perfect post-A-level present. He was also there for me (as were all my godparents) when my father died. I was 26 and in shock. It was having my father's closest friends around me that mattered most. They had been to school and/or university with him and knew him in a way that his sisters and ex-wives did not. It is lucky that we all like each other — there's no guarantee of that — but it's not just blind luck: my godparents all put in the work, in their different ways, and those relationships gathered momentum.

For the most part, people are still content to celebrate these relationships in the form of small silver objects — Tiffany carries silver spoons and rattles as though the 19th century never ended — but in the increasingly evolved world of "spiritual guidance" there is a growing vacancy for the GPF (guide, philosopher and friend) and a trend for "naming ceremonies". At Ludo's blessing, the artist godmother gave a speech about meerkats. Caregiving females, she said, risk their lives to babysit the pups of dominant females, in an example of altruism in the animal kingdom. This was now her role, she continued. And it's true, agreeing to be godparent is an act of great generosity. But the thing about children is that they give back. Lucy, another of Ludo's godmothers, has several godchildren. "It's a joy," she says, "and a way of keeping up with the young. I love watching the changes at each age, seeing what they morph into."

Making life

life

better

6.

It is always the little things...

Bar soap

By Emily King

As solid soap is increasingly replaced by liquids sold in plastic pump dispensers, it becomes ever more apparent that bar soap is design perfection by comparison. Why substitute a cumbersome bottle of slime for something that holds its own when unpackaged and whose form is ideal for both use and storage? Not only is a plastic container unnecessary, it prevents soap from contributing to the subtle scent spectrum of a home. In the public sphere, where soap touches the hands of the unrelated many, perhaps liquid has its place, but domestically, bars just make so much more sense.

In her 1932 children's classic *Little House in the Big Woods*, Laura Ingalls Wilder describes her mother making soap from cooking grease and ash. The technology may have moved on from that of late 19th-century Wisconsin, but the principles remain the same. The active ingredient in all soaps is a surfactant that interacts with water, creating a foam that removes grease and dirt from an object. (These days, your bar is unlikely to be made from leftover bacon, unless you're hanging out with radical survivalists.)

Soap may be a mild substance, but it provokes passion. Changes of formula inspire outrage, and discontinued lines prompt fanatics to hunt out hidden stashes. In the UK and North America, the most iconic soap of yesteryear was Pears, the amber oval with the strange, cake-like aroma. The brand still exists, but the bar has been reworked beyond all recognition, losing its lovely concave shape and distinctive scent. Now it's just one of a number of translucent varieties that the uninitiated might refer to as glycerine soaps. Closer investigation reveals that glycerine is a by-product of all soap-making and that translucency is a sort of styling feature, the result of an additional process involving sugar and alcohol, which can be drying to the skin.

Today, the bar that attracts the most rave reviews is the cheap and cheerful Dove, but if you're willing to experiment, there are many more sophisticated options to try. For those who welcome the longevity of a high-quality soap and are suckers for the crisp logotype its density permits, let me recommend Eau du Soir by Sisley. More suitable for the body than the face, with a rich concentration of the company's signature chypre fragrance, it wears down to a perfect wafer-thin disc — a small, slippery ideal until the very last encounter.

Inside pocket

By Susan Irvine

We wear the trousers, we've burned the bras, the high heels are strictly optional and nobody under 50 has even heard of a Playtex 18 Hour girdle, so how is it that a century after female suffrage we still lack an essential element of post-patriarchal dress?

Ladies, there's an elephant in the changing room: the inside pocket. This is the pocket of liberty, the pocket of financial independence, the pocket that no man on earth would ever be without in his jacket. It's designed first and foremost for safe stowage of a wallet. Yet 99 per cent of jackets made for women do not have one. (And, designers, don't complain that women have breasts. Men's bodies are no more streamlined in their own way and it didn't stop trousers being invented.)

For stowing serious stuff, women are expected to drag a bag around, something external to the body, prone to be left behind; something, to my mind, as hobbling as five-inch bootees. I have nothing against five-inch bootees, but for everyday, you want flats. And an inside pocket.

But while sneakers are everywhere, an inside pocket is still a chimera in female fashion.

Only one designer has ever understood this. Helmut Lang. Understandably, though unbearably, he gave up fashion for art in 2005. I still have my Helmut Lang man-cut (and yet not) suit from the late 1990s, the jacket of which boasts not one but two inside pockets. This is like all your buses coming at once if you are into pockets. I can slip wallet, photo, smartphone, key, fountain pen, emergency chocolate and more into these pockets; I can saunter down the street hands-free as well as every other kind of free. That's lib.

And on PJs?

At first glance, an inside pocket on your PJs is a bit of a lobster telephone. Why would you need an inside pocket on a garment you will be wearing not only indoors but in bed? But think again. What could be more intimate? In this pocket, you will stow the one thing you must always have about your person. OK, condom if you must. But I feel it should be something closer to your heart. Especially if it goes in the inside pocket of the inside pocket — which,

remarkably, the Gentlewoman/ Tekla pyjama also has. This inner chamber could shelter your migraine pill, a lock of your little boy's hair, Rilke, a scrap to write your dreams on.

Some years ago, my husband, who is Jewish, gave me a slender gold ingot in a tiny tartan envelope. Put that in your shoe, he told me, for when you have to run. I didn't put it in my shoe; I keep it by my bed. But that's not good enough. Because when the thought police, or whoever it's going to be in the future, come knocking, you need to jump without thinking, out of the bedroom window and down the road, supplied with love, poetry and the ultimate cashable object all in one sliver stowed next to your heart. That's what I'd keep in the inside pocket of the inside pocket of my PJs. Whatever you plan to keep in yours, make sure that in one way or another it's worth its weight in gold.

Small pour

By Marina O'Loughlin

I love a half glass of wine, a shallow, fragrant pool at the bottom of the bowl. I first came to appreciate the joys of restrained quantities of wine served in good glassware when I was fortunate enough to score a table at Catalonia's El Bulli in 2009. The parade of courses at this legendary (now sadly closed) restaurant was so numerous that to accompany them with fuller glasses would have required the installation of a vomitorium. But the elegance of the small servings was notable, underlining the fact that this was food and drink to really absorb and be bewitched by — not a blowout or what the *Beano* used to call a "slap-up feast". From then on, a judicious more-than-a-splash at the base of a glass was known in my house as "the Bulli pour".

There are functional benefits to the half glass, too: white wine doesn't get warm; varietals can breathe properly, releasing the full, glorious complexity of their characters; and you can try a dizzying number without getting too dizzy. So the arrival of the Enomatic machine — a new technology that uses inert gas to allow a bottle to be dispensed in small quantities without spoiling — in independent merchants was, to this oenophile, like letting a child loose in the sweetie shop.

I will cross cities for a small pour served in insanely delicate Zalto glassware — imagine the difference between regular sheets and lofty-thread-count linen and you'll get the general idea — which is what they use at my beloved Noble Rot in Bloomsbury (in which, full disclosure, I have a small involvement). Their 75ml measure — as opposed to the normal pub "small" glass at 125ml and made possible by the revolutionary Coravin system that miraculously extracts wine from a bottle without popping the cork — is the height of restrained luxury. The glass is simply more seductive when less than half full.

High time

The era of the smokeless high is upon us as an intoxicating class of products emerges, along with a new group of female consumers who like their marijuana lab-tested, low-dosage and ideally edible.

By Ann Friedman

I was in my doctor's office, filling out forms for a routine physical check-up, when a question stumped me. Do you smoke marijuana? The answer, technically, is no. But that's more of a half-truth. The full truth is that you don't need to smoke to get high any more — my doctor should probably update her paperwork.

In January 2018, recreational cannabis became legal in California, where I live. As in 15 other states and Washington, DC, people here can purchase marijuana products and consume them for pleasure. With legalisation, more of us are getting high than ever before. But often there is no smoking involved. We place a tiny mint on the centre of our tongue. We nibble a square of organic chocolate. We slather ourselves with infused oil.

The smokeless high is a far cry from the stinky world of skunk weed and novelty pipes, and it's particularly appealing to those of us outside the stereotypical stoner set. In 2009, *Marie Claire* coined the term "stiletto stoners" to describe women who relaxed with a joint rather than a glass of Cabernet after a long working day. And though I have never been the type to wear stilettos, the term could have applied to me back then. But things have changed quite a bit since then.

The cannabis plant can be split into several different active compounds, including the psychoactive THC (tetrahydrocannabinol), which gets you high, and the non-psychoactive CBD (cannabidiol), which users say has more of a body-calming effect. Until recently, CBD-potent strains weren't widely available, but legalisation has expanded the number of cannabis products that appeal to a wider market than just heavy stoners. Some of the most popular modern iterations of high-grade grass are not intended for smoking — among my favourites are super-low-dose edibles and an under-tongue spray, both of which contain a combination of THC and CBD.

Trying to describe the particular qualities of a drug experience will make even the most astute writer sound like Martha Stewart trying to banter with Snoop Dogg. But I will say this: there is a real ease to a smokeless dose of cannabis. Enjoying a low-dose mint is not unlike the pleasant buzz I feel after two glasses of wine or a single generous pour of whiskey. You won't find me consuming weed chocolates or CBD tinctures at a rollicking party, though. They are for winding down in the bath, enhancing a cinema experience or enjoying a walk in the park. If you opt for a low dosage and get it right, it's probable that no one but you will ever know you're stoned. You'll simply be calmer, quicker to laugh and, depending on the cannabis strain, a more sensual or creative version of yourself.

Yet I didn't always have an easy relationship with edibles. They can take anywhere from 90 minutes to two hours to take effect — the time determined by your body and how much you've had to eat that day — so if you accidentally take too much, you don't know until it's too late. (Smoking and vaping, by contrast, result in an instantaneous high.) A few years ago, I consumed a larger-than-advisable portion of a pot brownie on the night before an appointment with my optician and barely survived the eye test with my wits intact. I swore off edibles. But as weed has become widely legalised and culturally acceptable (at least for people of a certain race and income level — others, it should be noted, are still serving ludicrously long prison sentences for selling and consuming this now-normalised drug), the range of professionally produced edibles has started to change my mind.

My dispensary of choice was previously quite strict, requiring a medical card — which I've had since my first visit to a dubious establishment called DOC 420 a number of years ago — and a referral from an existing member. It is now open to the general public. And the budtenders, the friendly concierges who help you select cannabis products, often reply apologetically that they are sold out of everything I like — including Petra mints by Kiva and Care by Design's sublingual spray, which is one of the best menstrual-cramp remedies I've ever found. Clearly, I'm not the only one who's come around to edibles.

The popular appeal of edibles makes sense when you consider that legal weed markets tend to coincide with places where consumers are obsessed with wellness and sceptical of pharmaceuticals. I know many women who take cannabis quasi-medicinally. Why pop a painkiller to relieve a headache when you can massage some CBD balm on your temples? A friend of mine who has two young children refers to the cannabis-infused chocolate chip cookies she nibbles at the end of a long day of childcare as "mother's little helper" — a gentler and less addictive alternative to an older generation's benzos. Another friend uses a combination mint to reduce her anxiety on long flights.

"Legalisation always creates consumers who are new to cannabis, and their profiles and habits stand apart," BDS Analytics, a company that tracks trends in the market, reported at the time. It went on to say that newcomers tend to prefer edibles to smoking, and most want to start with very low doses. And these newbies are, for the most part, women aged between 25 and 44. The new class of edibles has an Instagram-friendly aesthetic that appeals to this demographic. They're sold through websites with clean, minimal design — all pastel backgrounds and knowing copywriting. The brand Lord Jones promotes itself slyly as "for your royal highness", for example.

Gone are the days when getting stoned meant tie-dye prints and black-light posters. Companies such as Défoncé Chocolatier and Pot d'Huile, a maker of cannabis-infused olive oil, wrap their products in matte black labels that wouldn't look amiss in Fauchon. New body-care brands are also finding their market. With cannabis brands mimicking mainstream design trends, it's no surprise that high-street labels such as Milk Makeup, which makes a mascara with CBD oil — "One hit for high volume" — have begun dabbling in dosing too. As legalisation spreads, it's easy to imagine every beauty brand adding a line of cannabis-infused luxury products, with prices to match. CBD hits a marketing sweet spot: it's legal but still edgy, indulgent but natural. Even old-fashioned consumers who still prefer to smoke their marijuana have probably noticed an aesthetic shift.

When I asked my friend Amanda Chicago Lewis, a reporter who covers the cannabis industry, about the proliferation of lower-dose, aspirationally packaged products, she explained that this is a sign that the market has matured. In places where marijuana is semi-legal — sanctioned for medical but not commercial use, say — the products tend to be sold with homemade labels in Rastafarian colours, dubious dosage information and silly names that reference more famous products stereotypically consumed by stoners ("Weedos" instead of Cheetos, perhaps). And often the only available edibles contain enough drug to tranquillise an elephant — or satisfy a lifelong stoner with a formidable tolerance. In states that regulate the market tightly, consumers still buy the devil's lettuce illegally, from guys on bikes. The dark ages! But as cannabis transitions to full legality in a region, testing labs spring up, making it possible for manufacturers to determine a product's exact potency and to sell edibles with consistent dosages.

And so the era of the low-dose high is upon us — and not just for cannabis. A writer in *The New York Times Magazine* joked that microdosing LSD and psilocybin mush-rooms at work has become more acceptable than ordering a cocktail at a lunch meeting. Especially in the tech sector, tiny amounts of psychedelics are perceived as improving productivity. But low-dose cannabis edibles appeal to me for the opposite reason. I enjoy them precisely because they make it difficult to worry about meetings and emails. In fact, I'm writing this several days past my deadline be-cause I tried to compose the initial draft while in the loose grip of an edibles high. After the mint kicked in, I was quick to follow my ever-present deadline impulse to stand up from my desk, leave my laptop behind and take a lazy walk through a nearby park. It wasn't that I was catatonic and *unable* to work — as with my unfortunate brownie inci-dent — it's that I was able easily to convince myself of the value of taking a break. Such is the oxymoronic appeal of the low-key high.

The black napkin

By Caroline Roux

Many visitors to smart restaurants arrive dressed in dark colours. Among my no-brainer dining looks are a black Jil Sander dress (A/W 2011) in a wool so slick it looks like neoprene and a black silk McQueen pencil skirt of possibly 15 seasons' vintage. But however beautiful the fabric of their apparel, whether soft linen or velvety corduroy, and however dark the hue, every guest is given a napkin of linty white linen. Whatever sartorial precision has preceded the meal, the diner still leaves the table — a few pence lighter and a few pounds heavier — with an unfortunate white bloom on his or her carefully selected garment. Even the tablecloth can play a part, depositing further white flecks onto a deep-coloured dress, skirt or trouser.

A quick hand brushing won't remove them. A visit to the bathroom will only work if it's staffed by an old-school attendant with a nice stiff brush or a Mr Sticky lint roller, or it's equipped with hand towels just cottony enough to remove the offending fluff when lightly dampened. And suppose the diner is moving on to a nightclub, where UV lights turn lint into a lurid green haze? Or a late-night bar where the dusting of white might be taken for a light fall of dandruff or a case of eczema?

At the Delaunay in London's Aldwych (sister restaurant to the Piccadilly celebrity catch-all the Wolseley), the fleet of pearl-wearing waitresses can provide black napkins to help diners get round the situation. "We get about 20 or 30 a day in our laundry, and they are available on request," says the Delaunay's general manager. Such attention to detail is thrilling and comforting. In any part of the dining experience — food, service, décor — nothing's more enjoyable than a seamless marriage of style and substance. And what works better than black on black?

Umbrella

By Richard O'Mahony

In the hierarchy of fashion investments, the umbrella doesn't rank very highly, which is curious considering that plenty of fashionable cities (London, New York and Tokyo, for starters) see a great deal of rain. But the umbrella is largely viewed these days as a disposable item, its reputation tarnished by the near-universally experienced humiliation that is wrestling with a flimsy mess of rickety wire and torn nylon in the battering wind and rain.

Its status is that of something almost guaranteed to end up languishing in a cab or dustbin once the rain has stopped.

There is also, perhaps, a direct correlation between an umbrella's disposability and its cost — the cheaper the umbrella, the more likely it is to be lost, discarded or abandoned. When, for example, did you last lose your most expensive pair of sunglasses? Even in the fuggiest of festivities, you're not forgetting those Tom Fords. So why don't we seek out a better class of umbrella?

A good umbrella — found in places such as James Smith & Sons in London, Fox Umbrellas in Croydon, Ombrelli Maglia in Milan or Vienna's Wilhelm Jungmann und Neffe — has a sturdy steel frame with a slim shaft either in hardwood, such as ash, or metal. From this protrude eight spokes (or ribs), over which a taut quality fabric with a waterproof coating is stretched. The hallmark of a truly smart model lies in the sound of the snap enclosure (aka the hand spring and top spring): the deeper the snap, the better.

Another audible pleasure is that of the rain beating against the cloth when the umbrella is at full mast; ideally a gentle, deep tapping — a sort of "puh-puh-puh" that can bring comfort and security to a dank November's day. And therein lies another delight of the umbrella: if it is full-sized, why not invite someone else in too? The romance should never be overshadowed by its practicality. *Les Parapluies de Cherbourg* would have been robbed of its charming plot device had it been set in Sunglass Hut.

When at ease, a quality umbrella can be a fabulous sight to behold. Rolled into perfect pleats, it's an exquisite artefact, exuding that indefinable whiff of expensiveness. Choose a crook handle so that it can rest conveniently on the wrist or at the elbow. If that's a bit too Mary Poppins, then a firm grasp midway down the shaft is advised, and a straighter back and a more purposeful stride may well result.

The flippancies of fashion dictate that at some point even "investment" accessories will be superseded by newer, have-to-have-it-right-now versions. But a good umbrella, barring an extreme act of nature, will remain a glorious marriage of elegance and utility for seasons to come.

Telephone

By Caroline Roux

Not so long ago, the telephone went out of favour. There was email (businesslike!), texting (brief!), Facebook (modern, with pictures!), Twitter (even briefer and more modern!). And for those seeking an antidote to things digital, there was the ladylike pursuit of letter writing and the charm of the postcard — communication's equivalents of embroidery and home baking.

But those emails pile up, don't they? It requires a 500-word opus to convey what could be said in a minute. And you're left waiting around for a reply. Facebook is a window into a world too many. It can take a 10-text volley just to set up a cinema date. And tweeting? It's the etiolation of language, unless handled with care.

Swift, smart and (it is to be hoped) confidential, making a phone call has never felt like a better option. There's no Bcc

---

Making life better

function, no risk of sending an aside to the wrong recipient and — what joy — a real person at the other end. It might be a triumph of technology to be able to watch a film on a smartphone on the tube, but what could be cleverer than being able to hear someone's voice in your ear at the click of a button, even if they're on a beach in Rio and you're in a bar in Moscow? A phone call has the intimacy of listening to the radio; the imagination can provide the pictures.

In 1970s London, it was considered the height of chic to have a sturdy cream telephone sitting on one's floor, as seen in David Hockney's period-piece portrait "Mr and Mrs Clark and Percy". The usual response to its ring was to light a cigarette, then pick up. There was no mid-conversation ambulation. The phone was plugged into the wall. The experience was exclusive.

While the instrument and the ritual have changed, phoning's range of purpose — from making a 20-second confirmation of an arrangement to having a conversation long enough to replace a dinner date — has not. At lunch recently I sat between two women of distinction in the worlds of art and retail — you would know them both by name. While both had staff to do their tweeting and used texts to communicate with their children, they were most excited about their recent rediscovery of the telephone. The instrument they'd found intrusive at its (pre-text) peak they now saw as uniquely efficient, courteous and fuss-free. And I bet they get a little thrill out of surprising the caller each time they pick up.

Chill with ice

By Richard O'Mahony

Here's a culinary ruse that anyone who's ever lifted a spoonful of bran flakes to their mouth expecting a cool crunch and instead encountered a lukewarm squelch will truly appreciate: next time, pop an ice cube into your bowl. But diluted milk? Yeuch! Sidestepping this watery fate depends on the size and density of the cube: a larger one will melt more slowly, keeping the milk chilled and creamy. Cereal satisfaction! A hefty block can easily be forged in your freezer at home; there's no need for an industrial-strength ice machine (though if you're so inclined, the Clinebell CB300X2E is the daddy). Perfect cubes can be yours with a silicone tray featuring two-inch square compartments. An extra safeguard against dilution: why not make them out of the liquid in which they will be deposited? This method has a particularly cheery effect when applied to wine and spirits. Salud, honey!

The un-

7.

mention-
ables

It might seem as if nothing is taboo in the 21st century. But some subjects still make us squirm. They often involve money, but might also include drugs and blood. And evoke no end of shame.

Menstrual cup

Long mired in shame, periods are up for discussion at last. While the attitude is modern, the paraphernalia remains unchanged, with a majority of women locked into the tampon/pad binary month after month. Consider instead the menstrual cup. As Ann Friedman discovers, a closer look reveals environmental — and health — benefits we've been ignoring for decades.

I stood with one leg up on the bath, the other planted on the cold tile floor. My knees wavered, sweat dotted my upper lip. *Just breathe*, I told myself. *Relax*. I didn't have a choice, really. A pandemic was raging outside; no A&E doctor was going to take the time to remove this menstrual cup from my body. I took a deep breath and tried again.

Here I was, nearly 40 years old and having what felt suspiciously like a coming-of-age moment. As I tried to get a grip on the bell-shaped silicone cup, I recalled the first time I put in a tampon. The unhelpful diagrams. The sneaking suspicion I was not doing it right. The rising panic. The fear — and awe — that my body was a vast universe unto itself, with many unexplored corners where things could get lost if they weren't precisely accounted for. I'd been a tampon user ever since.

Throughout the 20th century, the cultural consensus about periods was that they were inconvenient at best, shameful at worst. Even the language — "feminine hygiene", "sanitary products" — implied that there was something inherently unclean about monthly blood, which was best disposed of using a floral-scented, plastic-wrapped device. Outwardly, I laughed at tampon ads in which smiling women in tight white outfits frolicked on beaches, but I was secretly seduced by their promise.

For most of my life, all I've wanted is to get through those five days each month with the least possible pain, mess and visibility. What could be more horrifying than the world knowing that your insides are leaking out? Once, as a teenager, when I was surprised by my period at school, I had to turn to the coin-operated maxi-pad machine in the girls' loos. I spent the rest of the day with what felt like an inflatable mattress between my legs, fretting that my classmates would notice my slight waddle. At least I hadn't stained my clothes.

I was a voracious reader of teen magazines, so I lived in fear that a boy (always the cutest in school) would point out a red stain on the seat of my trousers. And while I was too scared to watch horror films, I had absorbed the plot of *Carrie* by osmosis: failure to successfully hide one's period could result in bullying, ostracisation, even death. It's no wonder I settled on the applicator-free tampon — it could be easily concealed in the palm of my hand, worn internally and then flushed away. Almost as if I wasn't bleeding at all.

Several decades into my menstruating life, I began to realise that discretion was no longer important and disposability was less than ideal. Trapped at home, I was re-evaluating nearly every mundane aspect of my life: was now the time to try something new in the period department? Enter the increasingly popular menstrual cup.

As I found out when I asked around, the cup has its evangelists. Many of my friends had never tried it, but the ones who had were devoted. One was on the verge of tears as she told me how much she loved her DivaCup. She wasn't grossed out by the idea of collecting her blood — in fact, she had become fascinated with noting its different colours and consistencies to assess her uterine health as she moved through her cycle. "But," I asked, "what do you do when you're out in public and your cup runneth over?" I could not envision how she exited the cubicle, made her way to the sink to wash the cup and then returned to the cubicle to reinsert it. She simply emptied it into the loo and put it back in, she said, but it wasn't often an issue: whereas a tampon must be changed every four to eight hours, cup users can go up to 12 hours without having to empty it. In fact, in terms of volume, the average menstrual cup holds about twice that of a regular tampon, at 20ml (some cups hold double that volume).

Other friends touted the cost savings. Most women will menstruate for 40 years, on, according to Unicef, a total of some 3,000 days — more than eight years — and spend, on average, about £4,800 on menstrual products, Bloody Good Period reports. Equally importantly, the charity adds, a menstrual cup offers environmental benefits: each one is reusable for up to 10 years, saving the equivalent of 2,750 tampons from going into landfill or being flushed into the sea. The environmental charity City to Sea, using data collected by the Marine Conservation Society, found that menstrual products are the fifth most common single-use plastic items found on beaches, ranking above coffee cups and straws.

Engaging so directly with one's period used to be the province of ecologically minded hippies and feminist radicals. The vast majority of women, like me, picked a pad or tampon brand they could reliably find at their corner shop and stuck with it until menopause. It wasn't until 2015 that period-positive ideals started to reach the mainstream. Kiran Gandhi crossed the finishing line of the London Marathon with a blood-red triangle clearly visible between her legs. *Time* magazine declared Thinx period underwear one of the year's best inventions. Soon, a UK ad was using blood-red liquid instead of the traditional blue to showcase the absorbency of a menstrual pad.

Now "better period" products are receiving millions in start-up cash, and it is estimated that the global menstrual cup market will be worth $1.89 billion by 2026. The world's most successful cup, the Ontario-based DivaCup, is available in many local shops, next to the pads and tampons. In 2018, even Tampax released a reusable cup.

We've been building to this point for more than a century. Menstrual cups date from 1867, when a Chicago man named S. L. Hockert invented a sack-like "menstrual receiver" designed to be worn internally. The schematic drawings are positively medieval, and I am relieved to report that it was never manufactured. The earliest cup that would be recognisable to modern eyes was patented in the early 1930s by a group of American midwives. But the Second World War led to rubber shortages, which spelled the end of production for this rubber device. In 1959, the design was sold to Robert P. Oreck, who promoted it under the brand name Tassette. But that failed too, in part because, according to the online Museum of Menstruation, the words "vagina" and "period" were "almost forbidden to use in advertisement". There was another problem: women didn't want to deal with disposing of the blood and reinserting the cup. It took until 1987 for a menstrual cup to find modest success. Introduced by Lou Crawford of Cincinnati, Ohio, the latex Keeper was marketed to women who wanted to take charge of their bodies and save the earth. The difference wasn't technology, it was feminism. The Keeper is still in production today. By the time I decided to give the cup a try, the number of options was dizzying — a 2019 survey by the *Lancet Public Health* medical journal found 199 different brands on the market.

Cups come in a variety of sizes, ranging from about 3cm to 6cm in length and 3.5cm to 5cm in diameter. The bell-shaped part is slightly different on each, and the stems have different shapes and lengths, too. They are made of latex, a kind of rubber called TPE or silicone, which protects the membranes of the vagina from the drying effect of tampons while also being hypo-allergenic, and they vary in firmness. Where does one even begin to figure out which to buy?

Luckily, one need not rely on word of mouth. There are several online quizzes to help the cup-curious find their perfect fit. I clicked on one and breezed through the first few questions: age, pregnancy history, exercise habits. Then I came to a question about cervix height and had to pause so I could take an approximate depth measurement — the most intimate act I have ever undertaken at the prompting of an online quiz. I ordered the site's top three recommended options, of varying size and firmness, then added rush shipping. According to my cycle-tracking app, I was cutting it close.

I wasn't exactly looking forward to my trial period. While I don't faint at the sight of blood, menstrual fluid is only about half blood: the other half is mostly endometrial tissue and cervical mucus. I did not love the notion of all of that just... sitting there, held in a cup within my body, for up to 12 hours. Then there was the matter of removing it — I'd read a few horror stories about the cup generating so much suction it pulled out IUDs. I thought back to something one of my friends had said: "I could just see myself having a Mr Bean moment with a cup of blood in a public bathroom, accidentally flinging it over the stall."

While I waited for my cups to arrive, I decided to discuss my anxieties with a professional. I called Erica Chidi, a health educator. "We are at an interesting point of peak awareness and peak curiosity about cups," she said. Yet they are not for everyone. "We can't shame women for not wanting to have high contact with their body because our culture has done nothing to support that." She suggested I try all three before I was bleeding. "Use some lubricant, place it inside, try the different folds." She was referring to the methods for inserting a menstrual cup so that it goes in smoothly and then opens inside the body to create a seal. Just don't try a cup for the first time before you leave for the office on a Monday morning, she advised.

I took to heart her gentle reminder that I wasn't just trying a new device: I was rewriting an aspect of my relationship with my own body. Learning to put in a tampon had represented the same thing; now I was levelling up. Or rather, going deeper. While the environmental and financial case for the menstrual cup provided motivation, ultimately I was most intrigued by my friend who had spoken rhapsodically about investigating the contents of her menstrual cup. I realised that I envied her ability to find not just peace but pleasure in this stigmatised bodily reality.

I am not alone in wanting to feel that pleasure. Where there was once money to be made by inducing insecurity around menstruation, there is money to be made through empowerment and environmentalism. Disposability was the essence of modernity when pads and tampons took off a century ago, but sustainability is now the ideology.

Money

Money talk and friends are a dangerous cock-tail we are told should never be mixed. But the writer Otegha Uwagba is out to shake things up with full fiscal transparency that will ensure prosperous futures and close bonds.

If there's one thing that's guaranteed to put a strain on a friendship (besides, say, falling into bed with a friend's partner), it's money. Or rather, having different amounts of it, and the conflicting attitudes that often accompany financial disparities. In my teens and student days, it felt as though everyone was on a reasonably level footing, eking out our student loans until the end of term and more worried about exam results than who had what, and how much of it. But as the years progress, the individual fortunes in most friendship groups are likely to diverge — careers accelerate and stall, salaries track accordingly and the choices people made in their early 20s come home to roost. These differences can fracture even the most solid of bonds.

My first experience of this was when I was 22. I quietly phased out a friend simply because I couldn't keep up with her appetite for whatever trendy cocktail spot or chi-chi new restaurant she wanted to try that week — easy enough for her to afford on her banker's salary, less so for yours truly, who was at the time temping as a receptionist. In hindsight, I realise it wasn't entirely her fault that our friendship broke down, or even really her fault at all. I hadn't yet mastered the art of setting boundaries with friends whose spending I couldn't match, and couldn't fathom the idea of saying "I can't afford that." Instead, I slowly stopped replying to her texts, which was both the easiest and the most cowardly way of handling the situation.

So, while I've never fallen out with a friend over money borrowed or owed, never bickered over a bill or been cheated out of cash by an acquaintance (at least to my knowledge), I have certainly lost friends because of money. And as my 20s unfolded and our respective circumstances diverged, I realised that if I wanted to insulate my friendships from the potentially corrosive effects of financial divides I would need to master how to tactfully broach the issue. I didn't want to repeat the mistakes of my youth — nor should you — so here, for your consideration, are a few of the rules I've since adopted.

The first law of financially compatible friendship is to resist the urge to count your friends' money, no matter how tempting or how much of it they seem to have. Aside from the fact that you never truly have the full picture of someone else's finances (who's to say those lavish holidays aren't funded by an ocean of credit card debt?), it will only make you feel wretched by comparison. Here I speak from bitter experience — in the past I have driven myself mad by jealously ogling a friend's designer wardrobe or trying to do the maths on their swish new flat.

If you do find yourself keeping company with those whose pockets are deeper than your own, the second piece of advice — and perhaps the most important I can offer — is to be honest about your circumstances, both with your friends and with yourself; self-delusion can be an expensive habit. You'll find that it isn't anywhere near as mortifying as you might think to say, "I'm afraid that's out of my budget. How about..." It can, in fact, be rather liberating to take control of the situation in this way, and it allows you to steer your friends towards options more in your comfort zone.

Still, you'd do well to prepare yourself for the possibility of losing a few of them over your admission of penury.

There will be some who simply don't want to adjust their lifestyle to accommodate yours or who feel embarrassed by your circumstances. But take heart — I can think of no better way to weed out those friends who are clearly not worth having.

More recently, as a result of those occasions when I have found myself the comparatively better-off party, I have realised that when two friends are financially mismatched, the burden of sensitivity really ought to fall on the wealthier friend. On a purely practical note, it is far easier to scale down your spending than it is to scale up.

So, if you are the friend with money, here are some notes on how to proceed. A degree of magnanimity is required. An occasional invitation to your cash-strapped pal for dinner — "my treat" — will rarely go unappreciated. The key to successfully executing such acts of generosity is to be gracious. Repeatedly reminding the other party who is footing the bill is about as chic as policing what is ordered. As is "jokingly" wincing at the bill when it arrives. Be assertive with the bill-paying, firmly nipping the usual "Oh, are you sure?" pas de deux in the bud. Have your wallet ready to go rather than rustling around in your bag for an interminable stretch — or, better still, settle up when your guest is in the powder room.

This discreet, decisive tack can be applied to most situations, whether you are offering to take a harried friend on a much-needed holiday or covering an unexpected expense, although no friend will thank you for being made to feel indebted. I have been on the receiving end of that, and it is as ugly as it sounds. Years ago, after falling out with someone, I received an email tallying up the various generosities she'd lavished on me during our friendship (these mostly consisted of trips to her family's second home, which, although kind, had cost her nothing). I momentarily considered asking for an itemised bill so I could pay her off and be free of her, as in a friendship divorce settlement.

Anyway, it's unimaginative to assume a great night out relies on sipping £20 martinis. A home-cooked meal that stretches on as long as the wine lasts is far more enjoyable than a two-hour restaurant sitting, at a fraction of the cost. More to the point, both parties can play host. Why not holiday with friends who are on a tight budget by substituting that blowout trip to St Barts with a cottage rental in the countryside? A Sunday morning walk with a Thermos flask is a fine substitute for an overpriced brunch — and there's no service charge for sitting and gossiping on a park bench (gossip being what brunch is for). There are always alternatives, and part of being a good friend is being willing to meet others at their comfort level.

It should also go without saying that it's crass to moan about your money worries to a friend whose problems are likely to far outstrip yours. Keep your gripes about the cost of your new kitchen extension away from the friend who has recently had their rent increased or their hours cut at work.

At the same time, I have found that it helps to be transparent about the source of one's good fortune, particularly if the source is some hidden advantage — a wealthy spouse, perhaps, or a sizeable inheritance. The rather old-fashioned idea that it is impolite to talk about money has been replaced by a new norm whereby it is impolite not to, particularly if doing so can help lift the yoke of self-comparison so many of us carry when it comes to money.

In all instances, empathy is paramount. We live in precarious times, so it's best to treat others as you would like to be treated should your own fortunes suddenly take a turn for the worse. Consider, also, how much better it will be to be remembered as the wise old friend who deftly steered the ship through these choppy waters than as the one who let an otherwise harmonious friendship wither on the vine.

Shame

By Gert Jonkers

As much as my siblings and I loved our family dogs, we were less than keen on taking Boris, Ted, Castro or Porky for that last walk of the day. Most of the time, the task fell to my mother. She did it ungrudgingly, and alone most of the time, but when in need of company she had one effective ploy: "Anybody fancy checking out the interiors round here?" she would enquire. This diversion interested me in particular since I dreamed of a future as an interior architect. And so Mum and I would do the rounds, arm in arm, shamelessly taking advantage of the good Dutch tradition of never closing one's curtains. With the lights on, we were granted gloriously unobstructed views of the cosy homesteads of our fellow citizens in Dordrecht in southern Holland.

And what a curious tradition it is! For why bother having curtains if one never closes them? Anthropologists puzzle over the whys and wherefores of this blatant exhibitionism. Is it connected to the legendary stinginess of the Dutch? Is what looks like a curtain in fact just a narrow swath of fabric that couldn't possibly stretch across the expanse of that other Dutch phenomenon, gigantic windows front and back? A more likely explanation relates to the Calvinist belief that God sees everything and that to try to hide a sin is useless. Those who keep their curtains open, their books on the table and their hands off each other evidently have nothing to be ashamed of, and so those who draw their curtains evidently do — it's kind of the opposite of the presumption of innocence as stated in Article 11 of the UN's Universal Declaration of Human Rights. Anyway, it gave my mother and me plenty to chuckle about.

I didn't end up working in architecture, but I still enjoy the occasional welcoming, unobstructed view into other people's homes, and I follow the no-curtain rule myself, too. It's easy for me, as I live high up with hardly any neighbouring spectators. But I also believe in the idea that shame is an exhausting emotion. What's there to be ashamed of? My internet browsing? The fact that it can take me an hour to get dressed? The mess, followed by a cleaning spree, followed by another mess? I embrace my habits even if they're bad; otherwise I should make an effort to change them.

To get back to the no-curtain rule: my neighbours would have to make a bit of an effort to see me walking around naked, but if they wish to, they can be my guest. As for the other way around, I believe that a room with an uninterrupted view grants clarity of mind. I find this makes room for new thoughts and experiences. And I recall a tip from some self-help book to spend a few minutes at night at the window, looking out, connecting with the world outside. How successful would that be with the curtains closed?

Of course, I recommend doing all this within reason. Philip Johnson's 1949 Glass House, a worthwhile day trip an hour from New York City, is indeed the transparent box its name suggests. But even the great Modernist architect cheated. First, he bought all the land around the house so there was nobody to peek at him, and also, the estate featured other buildings for when Johnson longed for a bit more shelter, so hey.

Ludwig Mies van der Rohe was more radical in his pursuit of total clarity when he built Farnsworth House, another legendary glass box, in Plano, Illinois, in 1951. He wasn't going to be living there himself, though, so there was no chance he'd feel exposed or ashamed of his exhibitionist dwelling and its lack of curtains. And in fact, the architect and his client, Dr Edith Farnsworth, fell out afterwards — perhaps because of a failed romance or the astronomical final budget, but especially because of the building's total lack of privacy, about which she later complained. "The truth is that in this house with its four walls of glass I feel like a prowling animal, always on the alert," Farnsworth told an interviewer. "Any arrangement of furniture becomes a major problem, because the house is transparent, like an X-ray."

So much for the "weekend hideaway" she had asked Mies to design. The house was so radical that it became a tourist attraction, with Dr Farnsworth as part of the display. She must have been proud at times of the Modernist monument she had ordered, but surely there are limits to anyone's exhibitionism. My mum and I would have loved it, of course.

Tipping

The unwritten rules of gratuities simultaneously baffle, intimidate and threaten to define us. But good service deserves its own reward, so find out what's fair.

By Eva Wiseman

One warm September evening some years ago, Humberto A. Taveras and his family ate a bad pizza. Quite how bad is not documented — there are no details in *Time* magazine or *The New York Times* about the quality of cheese or the depth of crust — but both reported on Taveras's subsequent arrest for leaving only a 10 per cent tip. The story resonates not just because of the image of a family fighting the system but because it speaks to every one of us who has ever slid the tip plate back with anything other than total confidence. Taveras and his wife and children had been dining in New York with another family, in a restaurant whose menu stated that an 18 per cent tip was mandatory for parties of six or more. The charge he faced for failing to leave the extra eight per cent was "theft of services". His case hinged, then, on this question: is tipping a voluntary way of rewarding excellent service, or is it quietly compulsory, an undeclared portion of the server's wages to be paid directly by the customer? What is a tip? And why does it make us anxious?

Tipping crept up on us. In the 17th century, guests at private London homes were expected to leave cash payments, "vails", for their host's servants, and coffee houses began leaving out tip bowls. One, apparently frequented by Samuel Pepys, had its bowl printed with the words 'To Insure Promptitude", and some historians claim "tip" is an acronym. When wealthy Americans brought the tradition home from Europe in the 1800s, *The New York Times*, writing in 1897, warned that many thought it was antithetical to American democratic ideals. But tipping persisted, and to abstain made you appear selfish, or worse, poor. Nothing much has changed.

There are no lessons at school on when to tip or how much. So how do we learn which services require tips? My mother, picking up coffee in London recently, was chased down the street by a waiter who deemed her tip too mean; I wouldn't have thought she needed to tip for a takeaway coffee at all. Tipping in restaurants and bars is norm-driven, simply part of the culture, but elsewhere — at the hairdresser, for example — it's done out of appreciation. Yet I remain in a high state of purse anxiety — leaving a café, I hope the tippee doesn't think I'm ungrateful. Leaving a hotel, I hope he doesn't think I'm patronising. Leaving a beauty salon, I hope she forgets everything she's seen and that those few hurriedly given notes will wipe the image of my upper thigh from her mind.

In the United States, where consumers pay some $26 billion a year in restaurant tips alone, expectations around gratuities are high, but the rewards are more transparent — if you tip continuously at American bars, the bartender not only serves you first but slips you free drinks. In many, if you don't tip for the first drink, you'll find you won't even be able to order a second. An American critic friend says he follows "a minimum 20 per cent rule. I held a series of food service jobs when I was in my teens and early 20s — the tip is often the lion's share of your income. Even with poor service, I tip towards the high end, because I have no idea what else is going on in the restaurant, and I rarely get baldly unpleasant service. Also, I am lazy and can remember the number 20 without struggling."

In Britain, of course, the rules are intertwined with those of class. Jo Bryant, an etiquette expert who worked for *Debrett's* for a decade, insists tipping is "a custom

that should be respected and carried out appropriately."
Appropriately? She breaks it down. "In UK restaurants,
you should tip 10 to 15 per cent. If the service is good but
the food is bad, still leave a tip, but make a complaint to
the manager. If the service is bad, adjust your tip accordingly. At the hairdresser, tip five to 10 per cent of the total
cost of your bill. Taxis? Ten per cent. Hotels, give bellboys
one unit of currency — pound, euro, et cetera — per case.
Give doormen one unit for calling you a cab; leave a tip
for housekeeping in the room. And at bars, add 10 per
cent for table or bar staff if service isn't included." But
crucially, she adds, "Don't be ostentatious or showy about
leaving a tip — and never offload your coppers."

When tipping, so intrinsic to our relationship with
money, makes us feel alternately worthy, guilty, successful
or scared, it's a relief to have guidelines, stated so defini-
tively, so devoid of doubt. Our lives have changed, but, it
seems, tipping etiquette has stayed the same.

So what does tipping culture reveal about a country?
A lot, thinks Lonely Planet author Ryan Ver Berkmoes. "Tipping in Japan is simply considered rude. A price is a price.
Why would you give extra? And handing someone a tip
might imply that their untipped service is inferior." Tips
in the Netherlands may be refused, but more often they
operate on a sliding scale. A large party might choose to
reduce the percentage in a restaurant, reasoning that the
gratuity is still a substantial sum overall. "Dutch society is
very egalitarian, and trying to be flash or put on airs is
something done in *other* countries," Ver Berkmoes says.
"When everyone is riding the same upright bicycles, there
are few class distinctions."

Tipping has never been required of locals in Muslim countries, but is rapidly making inroads in areas that rely on tourism. "From Morocco to Egypt to Dubai, you'll find plenty of tourism experiences where a tip is expected," Ver Berkmoes says. "Often this is tied to very low local wages and the hope that affluent tourists will share the wealth."

In Singapore, tipping is discouraged — the government believes it encourages corruption. Hungarians consider it impolite to leave cash on the table and hold discretion in higher regard than the size of the tip. In Italy, one per cent is considered fair, but tips aren't expected, and in Spain, you round up to the nearest euro. Until recently, Russians considered gratuities undignified, but with the growth of tourism in Moscow and St Petersburg, Western habits have been introduced and you're expected to tip the waiter on top of the service charge. With such varying expectations around the world, tipping signifies more than gratitude; it reveals who we are; it's about having a good grasp of the local language.

Most of us believe that the better the service is, the bigger people tip. But research doesn't back this up. The tips we give have, in fact, little to do with quality of experience. Michael Lynn, once a waiter at Pizza Hut and now a professor at the Cornell University School of Hotel Administration, has researched the psychology of tipping. "Studies have found, for example, that the amount of sunshine outside has as big an impact on the tips customers leave as the customer's ratings of service quality." He cites the work of the anthropologist George Foster, who says the act of tipping hinges on guilt — guilt at being waited on and having more fun than the person serving us.

Leaving a tip, Foster argues, is the diner paying for a waiter's after-work drink.

Comparing the types of services people tip for in different countries with personality tests on people of those nationalities, Lynn concludes that countries with more "extroverted" and "neurotic" people give tips for the greatest number of services and tip the largest amounts. "Extroverts are outgoing, dominating, social people," he says, and they see tipping as an incentive for the waiter to give them extra attention. Neurotics are prone to guilt and anxiety, so they tip more because of a perceived difference in status between themselves and the server: the service itself matters little.

A week after he was arrested, the charges against Taveras were dropped, despite the restaurant's owner reiterating to the press that he'd made the claim on behalf of the hard-working people who worked for him, not for himself. The district attorney said her decision determined that nobody could be forced to pay a gratuity. Mr Taveras, meanwhile, interviewed after his case had been dropped, told a reporter that he'd since dined at several restaurants, and, he said, he'd left some good tips.

What drugs can you not live without?

Just between friends: in 2013, 31 highly responsible gentlewoman disclosed the pills, potions and powders that get them through in a pinch.

BELLA FREUD (designer, London) likes to mix it up. "The French create the best pill mixtures," she says. Her combo du jour is aspirin with caffeine, arnica and gelsemium. "It gives a real kick. Aches and pains just evaporate."

KIM SION (art director, London) uses a battery of supplements: "spirulina to help boost my immune system, cinnamon to stop mid-afternoon sugar cravings, Pure-XP Glisodin for anti-ageing, New Chapter Bone Strength and Eskimo-3 fish oil, all washed down with a freshly squeezed juice."

KRISTINA SALEN (CFO, WWE, New York) is meticulous in her drug consumption. "I drink 700ml of green juice, prepared by my husband, and, when travelling, Pure Encapsulations' Athletic Pure Pack, which is six different pills in a convenient daily pouch. Then at night I take 300mg of PS 150 Phosphatidylserine to help me sleep."

JULIE VERHOEVEN (artist, London) declares her undying love for Nurofen. "The small liquid capsules are my favourite. They're so pretty, like jelly beans. I reach for them at the first hint of any ailment or annoyance." Her chemical romance concerns her, though. "I do get twitchy if I don't have any on me."

JOAN JULIET BUCK (writer and editor Rhinebeck, New York) says, "God bless Redoxon with zinc! I simply cannot do without it. It's expensive in New York but worth it, and since I don't drink orange juice, it gives me something orange in the morning."

MARGARET DABBS (podiatrist, London) uses SODzyme. "It's made from extracts of melon and is a brilliant anti-ageing supplement." She also suggests regular doses of glucosamine, "as it helps keep knees, ankles and, of course, feet supple."

AMANDA HARLECH (creative consultant and writer, Shropshire) is hooked on "beetroot juice, milky coffee from Leila's in Shoreditch and my chiropractor."

OLIVIA WILLIAMS (actor, London) justifies her stimulant of choice, the whiskey sour: "I think the egg white qualifies it as a health drink."

MELANIE ARNOLD (restaurateur, London) prefers a good meal to a pill. But should events turn overly epicurean, she reaches for Solpadeine. "Fizzy bubbles for the stomach and pain relief for the head — it's amazing!"

PENNY MARTIN (editor, London) is for the first time in 27 years able to get through the month without the box of ibuprofen she previously required to keep her "mind-altering" period pain at bay. "My naturopath, Eve Kalinik, recommended I eliminate dairy from my diet," she explains, "and since then I haven't needed a single tablet."

BRIX SMITH START (musician and TV presenter, London) carries a comprehensive stash of party favours to ensure a great night and no nasty morning after: "Three DAOsin to combat allergies to champagne, red wine and cheese; two Alka-Seltzer in case someone serves rich food; two Solpadeine and two Syndol — you'll sleep like a baby!"

MIRANDA JULY (artist, Los Angeles) confesses, "I hardly ever smoke pot, but I'm always planning to. It's on my list of things to do more, along with exercise."

REBEKKA BAY (creative director, Copenhagen) follows a classic regime of omegas 3, 6 and 9 interspersed with the occasional Emergen-C.

The unmentionables

PRINCESS JULIA (nightclub legend, London) has toned down her ways. "The only pill popping I do nowadays is taking painkillers for the occasional hangover — what has the world come to?"

MIKI ZANINI (stylist, Milan) uses a potassium, magnesium and mineral salts supplement. "I usually take one called Polase. It helps me get through the fatigue of hot Italian summers."

ROMY MADLEY CROFT (musician, London), as one third of a wildly successful band, knows that life can present many temptations. But, she confides, love is currently her only drug.

CECILIA ALEMANI (curator, New York) has been taking 3mg of melatonin every night for the past 15 years, "and I'm totally addicted". Also, she adds, "on occasion, if I can't sleep and I can't stand my husband, I take 15 drops of Lexotan. These and one pizza a week keep all the troubles away."

VALERIA NAPOLEONE (art collector, London) says no to needles and uses BioSil ch-OSA advanced collagen generator instead. "It boosts the production of collagen, which is at the core of beautiful skin and healthy hair and nails. It does require long-term commitment, though — a minimum of six months."

DELFINA DELETTREZ FENDI (jewellery designer, Rome) says that she is "constantly getting stopped at airports because of the stockpile of Cephyl I carry with me each time I return from Paris. It's a painkiller only available in France. And I always have my La Rapidita on me — a hangover pill, which a friend sends me from the Dominican Republic. It makes me very hungry, so then I usually eat some chocolate bars that I have in my bag — I'll be obese but alert!"

NINA GOLD (casting director, London) has kicked her habit — "I'm a very proud and possibly smug recovering caffeine addict" — and replaced it with a concoction that oozes good health. "Invented by my acupuncturist, it's a green sludgy brew that contains hemp, sesame, flax, pumpkin seed, goji berries, bee pollen, ginseng, maca, cocoa powder and barley grass, among other things. It's truly a wonder drug!"

PERNILLA OHRSTEDT (architect, London) likes a cocktail to take the edge off the day. "And I prefer to shake my own. Manhattans are practically a family tradition."

HOLLY BRUBACH (writer, Pittsburgh) got hooked on coconut kefir, a natural probiotic made from coconut water, on a trip to Los Angeles. "Now that I know about it, I cannot live without it."

KIRSTY WARK (broadcaster, Glasgow) finds that old habits die hard. "I follow my childhood routine — a daily Haliborange tablet and a spoonful of malt extract."

YASMIN LE BON (model, London) says, "I've been struggling with my energy levels for years. I'm nearly 50; things change. So every morning I take SAMe 400, which helps keep me reasonably level. I also take levothyroxine and a bioidentical form of progesterone; it's changed my life. And as soon as I read about green-lipped mussel supplements I had to have them." Even world-famous supermodels need a little pick-me-up now and then.

IMELDA BURKE (founder, Being Content, London) has a secret: Pure Synergy Superfood. "It's been around for more than 35 years, but it's still by no means mainstream. It contains everything from seaweeds, greens and grasses to freeze-dried fruits and sprouts and cultivated medicinal mushrooms, coveted for their life-extending, immunity-strengthening properties."

KARLA OTTO (PR, London) reveals the key to her famous composure as she manages fashion's whirligig. "I take rhodiola for extra adrenal support, and turmeric, which has anti-inflammatory and antioxidant properties. Gaia Herbs are incredible, and I recommend trying Stabilium — it's a natural extract from the blue ling fish containing polypeptides, fatty acids and antioxidants."

LUCY McKENZIE (artist, Brussels) confesses, "the best thing I ever did for my complexion was start taking the contraceptive pill. I also take evening primrose oil capsules to avoid PMT and period pain, along with a cranberry tablet and an iron supplement. Now my skin is ready for all the abuse it gets from fags and booze."

LOUISE NERI (director, Gagosian Gallery, New York) has some good advice for joints. "Following a hip replacement in 2011, I've been taking vitamin D3, calcium and omega 3 to help keep my bones dense, especially since my job entails frequent long-haul travel."

CLAUDIA GONSON (musician, New York) reports her latest fad is for magnesium. "Apparently it's great for mood stabilisation. I also drink a mixture of nettle, oats, oat straw and clover blossom. I've been taking it for four months, and I do feel more steady."

SISSEL TOLAAS (artist and perfumer, Berlin) is Norwegian. She takes Omega^3 of Norway fish oil. "I think it's because I'm homesick for the sea."

The quality of recreational drugs in London has declined so much in recent years that GOSHKA MACUGA (artist, London) thinks they're barely worth taking.

Drug of choice

One

8.

last thing...

Hello, goodbye

The ways of meeting and greeting and then saying adieu are surely second nature. Except, perhaps, when they're devices meant to put one in one's place.

By Lauren Collins

In North Carolina, where I was brought up, greetings were governed by a straightforward code: if you found yourself talking to someone you didn't know, you introduced yourself by name. Men were presented to women, guests to hosts, children to adults. When an older person entered the room, you stood up. You still do.

"Hello" became more complicated when, in my 30s, I moved to London, and then to Geneva. The hyper-friendly approach doesn't go over so well with Europeans, who are likely to be more creeped out than charmed by a stranger's habit of bounding over and sticking out her hand. But is it two kisses? (French?) Three? (Swiss?) The variations are so dizzying that there is a website, combiendebises.com, devoted to the question, and to that of what side of the face the kisser should start with. (The residents of the Vendée, in western France, for example, plump for four pecks and heavily favour a right-hand start; those in the neighbouring *département* of Deux-Sèvres favour a single kiss on the right.) In Paris, where I live now, an American recently admitted to having "no earthly idea" what to call the woman who has had her children over for lunch every other Tuesday for years. She had her number, of course — listed in her contacts as "*la maman de Camille et Margaux*". To ask her her own name had never seemed appropriate.

Greetings are primal. All cultures require some form of them, probably as some sort of evolutionary holdover. They are the first thing you learn in any foreign-language course. But the word "hello" dates only from 1827. According to the *Oxford English Dictionary*, it was first used as an interjection. "Hello, Jim! I'll tell you what." Thomas Edison introduced it to wider use in 1877, as the thing you should say when you picked up the telephone. (Alexander Graham Bell preferred "Ahoy", while the New Haven, Connecticut, telephone exchange, America's first in 1878, suggested "What is wanted?") Both the word and the gadget shook up the class system, allowing people who hadn't been formally introduced to talk to each other.

The ruling class will always manufacture manners to distinguish itself from the bourgeoisie. In non-kissing Britain, for instance, the going affectation is to say "Nice to see you" rather than "Nice to meet you", as a sort of self-inoculation against having forgotten a previous encounter. If we follow the writer and critic Henry Hitchings' distinction between manners (meant to put others at ease) and etiquette (meant to put them on guard), this is definitely etiquette: it suggests that its utterer is so grand, and meets so many people, that he couldn't possibly remember whether or not you've been one of them.

Even if you are going with a good not-that-old-fashioned "hello", there are rules. Should you say it when you walk into a meeting? Yes. A doctor's office? Probably. The tube? No. The sauna? Definitely not. These codes, I think, have something to do with ownership, with acknowledging that a space belongs to someone (or no one) and that you have entered it. This is why you might ignore whoever's behind the counter at a chain store but salute the proprietor of an independent shop. The "*Bonjour, Madame*" that one absolutely must utter when crossing the threshold of a *boulangerie* or a *librairie* is a little verbal curtsy. The idea that our "hellos" and "hiyas" and "how-d'you-dos" can be a form of modesty, an affirmation of another's claim to a territory, redeems even the goofiest "whasssssup".

A popular quote has it that goodbyes hurt the most when people leave without saying them. But the "French exit" — the English term for an unannounced getaway — may be undergoing a renaissance, the modern partygoer declining to say adieu to you and you and you before running to catch an Uber. (Uber is the best thing to happen to people with a limited tolerance for socialising since bad oysters.) This can be thought of as live-action ghosting — the process by which a person starts a relationship, decides to sever it and, rather than stating his intention, just disappears, never to answer another text. If there are people out there dumping their significant others without a word, then surely it's OK to tiptoe out of a hen do before the tequila shots come round again.

It is, actually. The more self-consciously festive the occasion, the more elective the farewell. Sometimes the most graceful way to say goodbye is not to say goodbye at all. (The astronaut Christa McAuliffe knew this. "I don't really want to say goodbye to any of you people," she said, ducking fanfare as she boarded the doomed Challenger space shuttle in 1986.) At a birthday party, a cocktail party, a book party, an opening, a launch or any other mill-around affair with more than 10 souls, you can in very good conscience abandon your half-drunk glass of wine on the nearest flat surface and go home and take a bath. Even *Debrett's* acknowledges the appeal of an unfussy getaway. "When the time comes to leave, make a decisive exit: don't loiter in the hallway, coat on, prevaricating," the chapter on entrances and exits declares. It also suggests that one "try to reverse through the door so that the last impression you give isn't of your back". Who knew?

Hello, goodbye

In the dwindling hours of a wedding, a quiet departure is positively advisable. To bother a bride and groom who've finally made it out onto the dance floor would be churlish, the interaction more about you than them. If more people took leave as elegantly as Russians — who have a tradition of sitting in silence for a moment with a traveller before he hits the road — I'd reconsider, but it can feel cheap shouting excuses across a loud room. So cut a few rugs. Listen to the toasts. And know that you are free to vaporise the second you hear the first note of "Brick House".

On the other hand, do not slink out of a seated event, no matter how many people there are or how glancingly you know them. Because even if you think you have got off scot-free — at a corporate event, say, where your host wouldn't know you if he saw you — you haven't. There will be a place card with your name written on it. The person you were supposed to be sitting next to will Google you, and never forget that you left her at Table 16 pretending to be captivated by the silent auction.

But far worse than leaving without saying goodbye is not leaving at all. Just after I moved to London, a couple I admired tremendously invited me to dinner. Actually, it was to a "kitchen supper", a term I had never heard. I arrived at 8 p.m. We ate prawn laksa, drank wine, finished dessert. Tea and coffee were served. We were having so much fun that my hosts raided their chocolate drawer. Then they fetched the box of *sfogliatine* that I'd brought. They talked at some length about the literary festival they would be driving to, with their young sons, very early the next morning. I was having a ball. Thank God, I thought, that I'm attuned to cultural differences, that I'm not coming off as one of those priggish, early-to-bed Americans. The couple began cleaning their kitchen. I wanted to make a good impression, so I drank some more wine. They finally got rid of me at 2 a.m. when they stuck a sci-fi novel in my hand and called a cab. I have not been to dinner, or supper, at their house again. I can actually barely think about it.

So how do we say an elegant goodbye, without slinking out or overstaying our welcome? A friend told me a story: several months ago, in the dining room of an Austrian hotel, an older couple was eating schnitzel. At the end of the evening, having finished their meal, they did a strange thing: they stood up and bid the entire room farewell. Unnecessary, but lovely — the best kind of goodnight.

Contributing writers

Joan Juliet Buck is an American novelist, critic, essayist and editor. She served as editor in chief of *Vogue Paris* from 1994 to 2001. Her profiles and essays have appeared in US *Vogue*, *Vanity Fair*, *The New Yorker* and *W*. She is also the author of two novels, *The Only Place to Be* and *Daughter of the Swan*, and a memoir, *The Price of Illusion*.

Lauren Collins is a staff writer at *The New Yorker*, where her subjects have included Michelle Obama, Donatella Versace, Emmanuel Macron, the refugee crisis and equal pay. Since 2015, she has been based in Paris. She is the author of *When in French: Love in a Second Language*, and is working on a second book, about a coup d'état perpetrated by white supremacists in Wilmington, North Carolina, in 1898.

Seb Emina is the editor in chief of *The Happy Reader*, the award-winning magazine created by Penguin Books and *Fantastic Man* (of which he is a former deputy editor). His writing on books, travel, food and art has appeared in publications such as *The New York Times*, *The Paris Review*, the *Financial Times* and the *Guardian*. He is the author of *The Breakfast Bible*, a breakfasters' compendium, and lives between Paris and London.

Ann Friedman is a journalist, the co-host of the podcast "Call Your Girlfriend" and co-author of *Big Friendship: How We Keep Each Other Close*. She also sends a popular weekly email newsletter. She lives in Los Angeles. Find her work at annfriedman.com.

Sophie Hastings is a freelance journalist, specialising in the international contemporary art scene. She began her journalism career in the rarefied offices of *Tatler* and *Harper's* magazines, before decamping to Paris (via south-east Asia). On returning to the UK, she became the features editor at *Art Review* and has since written for publications including the *Financial Times*, *GQ*, the *Guardian* and *The Times*.

Susan Irvine is the author of *Muse* and *Corpus* and a book about perfume called *Perfume*. She is a visiting lecturer at the Royal College of Art in London, where she teaches a course on using smell as material.

Gert Jonkers is a co-founder of The Gentlewoman, and the editor in chief of *Fantastic Man*. The youngest of six, Gert was born in Otterlo, in the exact centre of the Netherlands. His mother was a speech therapist, his father a minister for the Dutch reformed church. Gert has been writing about people, music, art and fashion since 1992 and currently lives in Amsterdam.

Emily King is a London-based design historian who works freelance as a writer, editor and curator. She has produced several books including monographs of the graphic designer Robert Brownjohn and the art director Peter Saville. Recent projects include guest curating the London Design Museum's 2020 "Designs of the Year" show and researching an upcoming exhibition about ornament for the Drawing Center in New York.

Penny Martin is the founder editor in chief of The Gentlewoman. Other long job titles she has held include the Rootstein Hopkins chair of fashion imagery at the London College of Fashion, University of the Arts London; editor in chief of Showstudio.com; curator of visual materials at the Fawcett Library; and curator at the National Museum of Photography, Film & Television.

Marina O'Loughlin, who for more than 20 years has lived her professional life in restaurants, is the multi award-winning critic of *The Sunday Times*. Not many people know what she looks like — which is the way she likes it.

Richard O'Mahony is an award-winning journalist and editor. Starting out his editorial career as an intern with The Gentlewoman in 2010 — fresh from Central Saint Martins — he gritted his teeth, rolled up his sleeves and powered ahead to become the magazine's senior editor. He is also a contributor to *Fantastic Man* and *COS* magazines.

Caroline Roux lives in central London and writes about contemporary art, architecture and design. She was the deputy editor of The Gentlewoman from 2011 to 2015. She is a regular contributor to the *Financial Times*, *The Telegraph*, *The Art Newspaper* and many other fine publications.

Susie Rushton is a writer and editor who has contributed to The Gentlewoman since its first issue in 2010, specialising in food and sport. After a start in fashion journalism at *The Independent* newspaper, Susie transferred away from the catwalk beat to cover general features, as a senior editor at *Porter*, British *Vogue* and *The Daily Telegraph*. She lives in Wimbledon, south-west London, with her family.

Mark Smith, London-born, Amsterdam-based, is a freelance journalist, who has edited diverse titles including *Time Out* Amsterdam, *COS* magazine, *HOUSE* and his school magazine, *The Leodiensian*, which was a hotbed of wild speculation and anonymous poetry. His features and celebrity interviews appear in titles including *The Times*, *The Observer Magazine*, *The Sunday Times* and *Elle*.

Anna-Marie Solowij made a false start in the Civil Service but that was eventually put right, and she began her magazine career at *Marie Claire* in 1988, followed by *Elle* and — ultimately — British *Vogue*, winning many awards along the way. In 2012, she co-founded BeautyMART and in 2015 BRANDstand Communications, the beauty PR agency where she is creative director. She is on the advisory board of the British Beauty Council.

Otegha Uwagba is a writer, speaker and the founder of Women Who, a platform for creative women that operated from 2016 to 2020. She has written three books, including *The Sunday Times* bestselling *Little Black Book: A Toolkit for Working Women*. In 2018, she was selected for the *Forbes'* 30 Under 30 media list.

Eva Wiseman is a writer and editor based in London. Her weekly column in *The Observer Magazine* covers subjects including gender, relationships, the internet and the various pains of being alive today. She is the agony aunt for British *Vogue*, a contributor to *The New York Times* and an interviewer whose recent subjects have included Sophie Calle, Paula Rego and Christine Baranski. She has a number of scripts in development.

Index

The articles in this book were originally published in
The Gentlewoman magazine

For subscriptions, back issues, membership and to sign up to
The Gentlewoman newsletter, please visit thegentlewoman.co.uk

Modern Manners
Instructions for living fabulously well

A collection of essays, articles and
new perspectives on old rules from
the fantastic women's magazine, The
Gentlewoman.

Edited by
Kathryn Holliday and Penny Martin

Designed by
Merel van den Berg

Project managed by
Antonia Webb

Many thanks to Veronica Ditting,
Gert Jonkers, Lucy Milligan, Richard
O'Mahony, Caroline Roux and Jop
van Bennekom for recognising that
whereas etiquette is meant to put
others on their guard, manners are
meant to put them at ease.

thegentlewoman.co.uk

You should seek medical advice in re-
lation to medicines and use only as directed by a healthcare professional.

Every reasonable effort has been
made to acknowledge the ownership
or copyright for material included
in this volume. Any errors that may
have occurred are inadvertent and
will be corrected in subsequent edi-
tions, provided notification is sent to
the publisher.

Published by Phaidon

Phaidon Press Limited
2 Cooperage Yard
London E15 2QR

Phaidon Press Inc.
65 Bleecker Street
New York NY 10012

phaidon.com

Commissioning editor:
Emilia Terragni

Project editor:
Sophie Hodgkin

Production controller:
Sarah Kramer

Printed in Belgium

First published in 2021
© 2021 Phaidon Press Limited

ISBN 978 1 83866 356 8

A CIP catalogue record for this book
is available from the British Library
and the Library of Congress.

All rights reserved. No part of this
publication may be reproduced,
stored in a retrieval system or trans-
mitted, in any form or by any means,
electronic, mechanical, photocopy-
ing, recording or otherwise, without
the written permission of The Gentlewoman and Phaidon Press Limited.

The modern world,

1.

4. How to be...

5. Good relations

6. Making life better

7. The unmentionables

8. One last thing...

Contents

In The Gentlewoman's first issue, an eminent expert on the etiquette of communications insisted that it was perfectly acceptable to send condolences by text rather than on the black-edged stationery that was once de rigueur. A decade on and many digital messages later, we are not so sure. Some situations require the sincerity of a real-world note, whatever colour its paper. And herein lies our fascination with manners: not with the rules themselves, necessarily, but their mutability. Noting changes to conventions and mastering them can be a passport to avoiding the worst and experiencing the best of the modern world.

Some of the essays and articles we have published on the politics and peculiarities of the ever-changing everyday appear in this book, bringing together new solutions to classic conundrums (how to drink at the bar, the rights and wrongs of a regifted present, the pointlessness of shame) and offering tips on more recent concerns (anonymity, autoreplies, spending your money elegantly).

The best advice often came from our community of curious gentlewoman readers. Please therefore find four lists of responses to such queries as: What do you give as a thank you? and What drugs can you not live without? Like the magazine itself and the female icons it features, these readers paint an optimistic picture of life lived fabulously well today.

Penny Martin, editor in chief
The Gentlewoman